CHINA, AFRICA, AND
OF THE INTERNET

ABOUT THE AUTHOR

Iginio Gagliardone teaches Media and Communication at the University of the Witwatersrand, South Africa, and is Associate Research Fellow in New Media and Human Rights in the Programme in Comparative Media Law and Policy (PCMLP), University of Oxford. He holds a PhD from the London School of Economics and Political Science and has been living between Italy, Ethiopia, the UK, and South Africa, researching the relationship between new media, political change, and human development, and exploring the emergence of distinctive models of the information society in the Global South. He has extensively published in communication, development studies, and African studies journals, and his work has been translated into Arabic, Chinese, French, and Italian. His most recent publications include *The Politics of Technology in Africa* and *Countering Online Hate Speech*.

CHINA, AFRICA, AND THE FUTURE OF THE INTERNET

Iginio Gagliardone

ZED

China, Africa, and the Future of the Internet was first published in 2019 by Zed Books Ltd, The Foundry, 17 Oval Way, London SE11 5RR, UK.

www.zedbooks.net

Typeset in Plantin and Kievit by Swales & Willis Ltd, Exeter, Devon
Index by Rohan Bolton
Cover design by Kika Sroka-Miller

ISBN 978-1-78360-523-1 hb
ISBN 978-1-78360-522-4 pb
ISBN 978-1-78360-524-8 pdf
ISBN 978-1-78360-525-5 epub
ISBN 978-1-78360-526-2 mobi

MIX
Paper from
responsible sources
FSC® C013604

Printed and bound by CPI Group (UK) Ltd, Croydon, CR0 4YY

To Carolina and Elisa

CONTENTS

ACKNOWLEDGMENTS

This book is the result of nearly a decade spent exploring China's increasing engagement with Africa's information societies. Its beginnings can be traced back to many, disparate, events that occurred when I was pursuing research on media and politics in Ethiopia for my previous book. Some were casual encounters with new actors who had begun to populate the complex landscape of telecommunications in Africa – from Huawei and ZTE employees working on telecommunication expansion projects, to experts of cybersecurity trying to detect the techniques used by African governments to spy on their citizens. I still remember my surprise when, after an interview with the CEO of Ethiopia's Telecommunication Corporation back in 2008, I took a wrong turn down the corridor and came to see that most other offices on the top floor were staffed not by Ethiopian, but by Chinese, engineers. My interest in the growing role of China in Africa's information space was furthered by conversations with individuals working for consultancy firms or think tanks headquartered in Europe or North America, who appeared so adamant that a greater Chinese engagement in ICTs would only lead to greater authoritarianism. Their overconfidence convinced me of the importance to begin collecting solid empirical evidence – rather than trying to articulate principled responses to their arguments – to explain what was actually happening on the ground.

In 2010, moved by the aspiration to create a shared framework to analyze new forms of Chinese engagement in Africa, and responding to what already appeared a very polarized debate, I co-organized with the Programme in Comparative Media Law and Policy (PCMLP) at the University of Oxford (and with the support of the Economic and Social Research Council – ESRC), a symposium that gathered scholars from China, Africa, Europe, and North America, where we collectively discussed complementary and competing approaches to understand the role China can have in shaping Africa's media systems. This spirit has continued to inspire the following, more structured and systematic, investigations into the nature and consequences of Chinese support to the development of ICTs in Africa. My work at Oxford was further supported by the British Academy, to which I am most grateful for investing in my research through a very generous fellowship, and by the Leverhulme Trust, which provided me with the opportunity to further expand my focus and explore how different processes might contribute to a progressive fragmentation of the Internet in Africa, and globally.

I am indebted to the many people who generously shared their time with me –politicians, activists, civil servants, academics, programmers, engineers, and journalists in Ethiopia, Kenya, Ghana, Rwanda, and other countries where I extended my research over the years. I am grateful to the colleagues who shared some parts of this journey with me: Frederick Goloba-Mutebi in our joint research in Rwanda, Daniel Nkrumah in Ghana, and Nicole Stremlau in Kenya and Ethiopia.

This book – and its span – also represented an opportunity to enter into conversation with exceptional individuals who have played an important role in shaping what is contained in the following pages. Monroe Price, Bob Wekesa, Yanqiu Zhang, Cobus Van Staden, Eric Olander, Winston Mano, Nikia Clarke, Miriam Driessen, Elsje Fourie, Herman Wasserman, Keith Breckenridge, Anbin Shi, Sharath Srinivasan, and Deborah Brautigam have all, at different points in time, contributed to support or challenge my ideas in ways that have had direct consequences on my research.

I am particularly grateful to Dane Dagenstain, Vivien Marsh, Emeka Umejei, and John Stremlau, who have been so kind to read different versions of the manuscript as it took shape and to offer invaluable advice. A special word of gratitude goes to my editor, Ken Barlow, who has been supportive and patient as we pushed the deadline of the book to accommodate new evidence and the unpredictability of life. I also want to thank Kim Walker, who kindly oversaw the latest stages of the book, and Zed Books as a whole for being a unique example of a publisher seeking to make knowledge accessible on complex and controversial issues.

On a more personal level, I am fortunate for having been able to share different phases of the research that led to this book with my family. I am grateful to my parents, who understood how even family visits had to accommodate time for pushing this project forward, also giving me the encouragement I needed in difficult moments. To Guido and Pia, for their curiosity towards new enquiries and new ideas. To Carolyn and John, for the many conversations we had as the book took shape, which often led to new readings, connections, and ideas.

The greatest joy came from my daughters, Carolina and Elisa, to whom this book is dedicated. This is the first book I wrote as a father, getting up earlier and earlier to make sure the manuscript would still come to life, without taking away any of the bright moments I could spend with them. As previous books, this one would also probably not exist without the support, ideas, and encouragement of my partner and fellow researcher, Nicole, with whom I look forward to sharing many other projects and ideas.

1 | CHINA AND THE SHAPING OF AFRICA'S INFORMATION SOCIETIES

At the turn of the millennium, a deep-rooted sense of optimism was associated with the power of the Internet to transform politics and society, opening up closed regimes and loosening the authoritarian grip over their citizens. US President Bill Clinton's speech at Johns Hopkins University in March 2000 was one of the clearest embodiments of this spirit. As he argued:

> In the new century, liberty will spread by cell phone and cable modem. [...] We know how much the Internet has changed America, and we are already an open society. Imagine how much it could change China. Now, there's no question China has been trying to crack down on the Internet – good luck. That's sort of like trying to nail Jello to the wall.[1]

"Nailing Jello to the wall" became a common reference in the following years to indicate how, contrary to Clinton and many others' expectations, the Chinese government managed to achieve exactly what was once thought to be impossible. While China's online population has grown to become the largest in the world, the government has continued to maintain a tight control over the Internet, preventing it from being used in ways that could lead to dramatic and unpredictable shifts in power. The government's strategy has proved so effective that only a decade later, expectations that the Internet would have changed China have turned into fears that China could transform the global Internet, exporting its model abroad. Ironically, it was Hillary Clinton, as Secretary of State during Barack Obama's first administration, who spelled out the new fears.

Some countries have erected electronic barriers that prevent their people from accessing portions of the world's networks. They've expunged words, names, and phrases from search engine results. They have violated the privacy of citizens who engage in non-violent political speech. [...] With the spread of these restrictive practices, a new information curtain is descending across much of the world.[2]

This shift is significant both from a conceptual and from a political point of view. While in an initial phase, technology was expected, unaided, to bring change to a closed society, the same technology was later reframed as a tool of foreign policy, something that had to be embedded into a broader strategy to produce the expected results. It was as if faith in the Internet – per se – had faded.

As Hillary Clinton continued, "On their own, new technologies do not take sides in the struggle for freedom and progress, but the United States does. We stand for a single Internet where all of humanity has equal access to knowledge and ideas." For some, this marked the beginning of a new Cold War over the Internet, where discourses on the good society have begun to be publicly and visibly asserted as part of a battle to define a new global order.[3] While the United States has framed its struggle as an extension of the First Amendment of the American Constitution, promoting the idea of one Internet as a way to extend fundamental freedoms globally, China has been accused of working to fragment the Internet and project a more authoritarian version of it.

But are these two camps so neatly distinct? Is the fight for Internet hegemony really a fight between the free and the unfree world? Or is this narrative, which has forced individuals and groups to take sides, obscuring other forces that are reshaping the global Internet? And is it preventing other ideas of the Internet from taking root?

It has become increasingly common for the two Internet superpowers to trade accusations, citing hypocrisy and a willingness to support the Internet simply to extend its sphere of influence, or denouncing the other's evisceration of the very principles that guided the evolution of the Internet, including the erosion of free-dom of expression and privacy. Some non-state actors – think thanks, research centers, international NGOs – have joined the debate, often letting preconceived ideas about how the United States or China would be likely to behave guide their conclusions and recommendations, contributing to a further polarization.

This book seeks to play a different game. It brings evidence from a continent where China has dramatically increased its pres-ence and influence, and where the Internet is still taking shape, both at the level of infrastructure and regulation, to empiri-cally examine the extent to which China is actually (re)shaping information societies in Africa, and what this may mean for the global Internet. It does not assume that China will seek to charm other countries into following its footsteps. Rather, it lets the analysis of a number of cases where China has sponsored or has become involved in large-scale projects illustrate what strategies China is deploying and what the consequences are. Neither does it assume that projects sponsored by countries boasting a free and open Internet will necessarily strengthen open and inclusive information societies as their outcome. Rather, it allows for the contradictions and inconsistencies of the agendas promoted by Western donors, especially as they become embroiled in local networks of technologies, discourses, and actors. By doing so, it becomes possible to appreciate how strategies and forces ema-nating from the East and from the West, rather than necessarily competing or canceling each other out, may actually overlap in concrete settings.

The focus of this book will be on information societies, as they evolve at the national level, responding to global influences as well as to unique local configurations of technology and poli-tics, but also as they connect, chaotically contributing to the creation of a global system of communication. The term infor-mation society is by no means self-explanatory. It has been at the center of numerous debates and has been used to refer to different transformations brought by information and commu-nication technologies (ICTs). ICTs is the term and concept I will be using throughout the book, as the network of technical artifacts – including mobile handsets, routers, software protocols, personal computers – that together facilitate the digital production and communication of information. Often the focus will be on one central technology – the Internet – that has emerged as a central node in this network.

As Frank Webster noted, to many scholars focusing on the transformations brought by ICTs, "it seems so obvious that we live in an information society that they blithely presume it is not necessary to clarify precisely what they mean by the concept."[4] And yet, despite numerous claims of the revolutionary power of the Internet, an increasing number of robust, empirically grounded studies have shown how the real impact of the information revolution is more modest than usually thought, even in the country, the United States, where the Internet first appeared.[5] In this book, I won't refer to the information society through the lenses of the impact of the Internet on the economy or on political life. It would be presumptuous to think of Ethiopia, a country whose economy still heavily relies on agriculture and whose politics is carried out through complex physical networks connecting the center with the peripheries of power, as an information society. My focus will instead be on the building blocks that are being laid down in each country to give life to emergent networks expanding the ways in which individuals and groups communicate – horizontally (among one another), vertically upwards (towards more powerful actors and institutions), and vertically downwards (towards audiences). What are the visions that circulate in a society when debates on the Internet emerge? Which visions are magnified, and which are marginalized? What actors have the upper hand when these visions are turned into reality? And which allies do these actors seek to realize their plans?

China and the African Internet: a simplified narrative

The strategies the Chinese government has developed to discipline domestic media, together with the tendency of Western donors to advance their own models when providing assistance, have created the expectation China will be a net exporter of authoritarianism.[6] Google's former CEO, Eric Schmidt, and US State

Department advisor Jared Cohen have accused China of causing the Internet to fracture into smaller pieces, some controlled by an alliance of democratic states and others by sophisticated autocracies.[7] In 2018, Schmidt doubled down his prediction, suggesting that in 10 or 15 years, users may have to operate on a bifurcated Internet.[8] Early assessments of China's expansion into African media and telecommunications have warned about China's "emphasis [...] on forming alliances that are anti-Western and on promoting an anti-Western media model to combat what the Chinese regularly portray as part of an imperialist plan to distort the truth,"[9] or have stressed how China's "charm offensive" in Africa can undermine Western interests on the continent.[10]

The narrative framing China as active promoter of its own alternative model of the Internet is powerful and seemingly convincing. It rests, however, on assumptions that have not been empirically tested and on a lack of engagement with what China has actually done in countries where it has begun contributing to the development of national information infrastructures.

The first supposition is that China would behave as Western countries have done when engaging with and seeking to influence other media systems. To be sure, referring to a unified Western strategy towards media development would be both confusing and inaccurate. In my experience teaching in Chinese and African universities, I learned how often the term "Western media" is invoked, as if anything like that actually existed. As if the Italian media under Prime Minister Silvio Berlusconi, where both public and private TV broadcasters were under the influence of one man, and the United Kingdom's many layers of checks and balances to shield public service broadcasting from government interference, responded to a similar logic.[11] Also, when providing assistance to the shaping of media systems in foreign countries, different Western donors have promoted substantially different strategies. These differences have been the most apparent in those cases when Western powers sought to ambitiously – and arrogantly – overhaul entire national media systems, as in post-Soviet Europe, Iraq, or Afghanistan.

There is an element, however, that has characterized the vast majority of media interventions promoted by Western countries on foreign soil. Each country, when elaborating a strategy to influence other media systems, has sought to build on and advocate their own media model, the one that historically emerged to shape the relationship between their citizens, journalists, public authorities, innovators, and private companies. This is how, for example, the United States and the United Kingdom clashed in Iraq, the former seeking to "create an environment in which multiple voices [could] be heard as an antidote to the Baathist regime's propaganda, [and] be an indicator of democratic governance or respect for 'human rights"[12] and the latter trying to "develop a viable media based upon its own experience with a state funded public broadcaster."[13] It is therefore hardly unthinkable that an emerging power with a rapidly increasing international exposure would follow a similar strategy, seeking to impose or at least advocate its own model. And yet, as this book suggests, interrogating numerous cases of Chinese support to the development of ICTs across the African continent – and many other scholars have similarly argued for other sectors – there is little trace of China seeking to adopt a blueprint based on its "model(s)."

The second element that has allowed a narrative of China as active exporter of an authoritarian version of the Internet to persist is based on a lack of empirical engagement with the projects and programs China has actually supported abroad. Scholarly attention towards China's expanding media footprint in Africa has significantly increased in the past few years, seeking to better understand and more accurately portray the nature and impact of Chinese media and media systems on the African continent.[14] There have been fewer questions asked about possible connections between the Chinese and the African Internets, or, when these questions have been asked, answers have been largely based on deductions emerging from the analysis of China's behavior on the stage of Internet governance[15] or on assumptions that relationships between China and its African partners would lead to more censorship and surveillance.[16] As this book illustrates, by examining China's engagement in the African ICT sector, as well as by comparatively analyzing the case of two democracies – Kenya and Ghana – and two autocracies – Ethiopia and Rwanda – with whom China has developed increasingly strong ties, answers emerging from the ground tend to be much less definite. They are also more helpful to understand why and how the Internet is actually changing, in Africa and globally, possibly eroding the moral high ground for those used to pointing fingers at specific actors, but also offering more solid foundations to envision the future of national and global information societies.

China and the African Internet: a more complex story

The narrative described above makes "agency" its most notable victim. It frames China as an all-powerful actor seeking to charm or convince its partners into adopting its model, or "corrupting" them along the way, as it introduces its technologies and strategies as part of ongoing projects. It conversely depicts African counterparts as unable or unwilling to resist. As Chapters 2 and 3 will illustrate, the reality is starkly different. China has demonstrated an incredible ability to fit into distinct projects developed by different African states, supporting nationally rooted visions of the information society, rather than promoting template approaches. This has meant aiding the aspirations of the governments of Ghana and Kenya to strengthen infrastructure and the capacity of the state to deliver services in a competitive environment, as well as sustaining the ambition of Ethiopian leaders to expand access under a monopoly, maintaining a tight control over communications.

African states, rather the being passive recipients of blueprints developed elsewhere, have demonstrated remarkable skills in making use of Beijing's openings in the ICT sector to bolster their own development projects. The greater availability of funds and expertise from China has also increased the ability to fight off other donors' conditionality. Some would argue this is a problem, as conditionality has also meant greater pressures to respect human rights and fundamental freedoms. I will get to that in a moment.

The expansion, rather than contraction, of "African agency" in the ICT sector as a result of new partnerships with China resonates with other, empirically grounded, studies.[17] Some of them have challenged the overall framing of the relationship between

China and Africa as "China–Africa." They have proposed a change of perspective, to consider "Africa–China" relations instead, paying due attention to the ability of each African state to develop unique ties and projects with China – as well as with other partners.[18] This change of perspective is important and can offer a fruitful terrain for more nuanced understandings to emerge, but it does not – and should not – represent the denouement of the story. The emphasis on African agency, while questioning simplistic narratives framing China as propagating its model in Africa, can be similarly deceiving when it comes to understanding which ideas and power relations have actually been promoted since China became a major player in the global ICT sector. China may be supporting locally rooted conceptions of the information society, but within national borders, whose agency in particular is China actually helping?

Can China thus be considered a benevolent partner, using, as other donors do, aid to support its foreign policy agenda, but ultimately respecting the visions and rights of its partners? Is its approach simply following from the principles of "win–win cooperation" and "friendly collaboration" that have become the slogans in China–Africa relations? Or is there a darker side to China's support of Africa's ambitions?

In January 2018, French newspaper *Le Monde* broke with a story accusing China of having been systematically hacking the African Union (AU) headquarters in Addis Ababa. As *Le Monde* wrote, for five years, each night – between midnight and 2 a.m. – something seemed to keep the AU servers unusually busy. The reason, according to the newspaper's sources, was that critical information was being routinely sent to servers in Shanghai, China.[19]

The story produced diametrically opposed responses. In Europe and in the United States, it was received with contentment, as evidence corroborating the many warnings by Western politicians, analysts, and pundits that China cannot be trusted.[20] The new AU building – a US$200 million gift from China to Africa – appeared in the end to be a gigantic Trojan Horse, used to gain leverage over African partners. African leaders and AU officials kept a relatively low profile. According to *Le Monde*, the

AU technical staff had discovered the breach a year earlier and hurried to replace the servers in the building, but no AU official came forward to publicly denounce the incident. Rwandan President Paul Kagame, serving as AU Chair at the time *Le Monde* published its investigation, downplayed the incident. Seemingly unaware of any hacking, he declared that in any case, he would not be "worried about being spied on in this building."[21]

China's response, on the contrary, was unusually strong. As Eric Olander, a regular commentator of China–Africa affairs, remarked, on this occasion China stepped out of the heavily scripted style usually adopted in handling international controversies. Rather than releasing the customary press release, China's ambassador to South Africa, Lin Songtian, went live on the national broadcaster to denounce the spying allegations.[22] He flagged *Le Monde*'s accusations as despicable – a word rarely used in Chinese diplomacy – and part of a Western plot to undermine China's image, treating the newspaper as an agent of the French state. This unusually assertive response, while revealing uneasiness towards the allegations, also marked a significant shift towards a more direct, and conflictual, communication strategy on the international stage.

Another element that makes the analysis of China's contribution to the shaping of African information societies more complex is that it is not happening in a void, but is interacting with myriad other processes that exist beyond China's own policies and programs. As I explain in Chapter 5, the more I sought answers to some of the questions highlighted above, the more I came across a different type of publicly embraced discourse, especially by heads of state and top-level bureaucrats, to justify some of the repressive measures that have become increasingly common across the continent, including Internet shutdowns and the boosting of surveillance. Apart from very isolated cases,[23] when repressive measures have been adopted or proposed in countries as diverse as Uganda, Nigeria, Kenya, or Cameroon, it has not been China that has been held up as an example in favor of such measures. Across the continent, it has been the United States-backed anti-terrorism agenda, and the related securitization of development, which have offered much more easily exploitable arguments to legitimize the repression of online communication and the persecution of Internet users.

The securitization of development and foreign policy that followed the attack to the Twin Towers in New York on September 11, 2001 has offered new opportunities to political elites to consolidate their grip on power, while seemingly responding to exhortations emanating from the international community. Especially in authoritarian regimes, anti-terrorism laws, while purportedly displaying solidarity with the fight against global terrorism, have often been used to incarcerate, silence, or threaten opponents. In the digital realm, the securitization agenda, and the ways in which it contradicts other priorities in foreign policy and development aid – including the promotion of human rights and fundamental freedoms – has created new ways for governments to boost their ability to censor and surveil while continuing to ostensibly display their commitment towards policies and ideas promoted in the West.

In countries such as Ethiopia, the combination of resources and discourses from the East and the West has led to the paradox of having some actors – the Chinese government and Chinese companies – quietly taking care of the material implementation of a highly centralized and securitized information space, and other actors – the United States, which has sought to combat Chinese influence both in Africa and in the digital realm – offering the discursive terrain for Ethiopian authorities to justify the creation of such a space.

As these examples indicate, there is nothing simple in the way in which China is – directly or indirectly – influencing information spaces in Africa, interacting with – exploiting? – policies advocated by some of its own opponents and quietly supporting allies in ways that defy common prejudices about China's behavior, but may have repercussions in the longer term. Hence the importance of not reverting to simplistic narratives, either accusing China of corrupting the global Internet or praising it for its reinvigoration of South–South cooperation in the information sector. Instead, we need to develop tools that allow us to understand China's role on its own terms and from the ground up.

The technopolitics of China in Africa

To study the specific ways in which Chinese involvement in the ICT sector may be influencing the shaping of Africa's information societies, this book comparatively analyzes the cases of two democracies – Kenya and Ghana – and two autocracies – Ethiopia and Rwanda – with whom China has increasingly deepened its engagement since the turn of the millennium. This strategy is aimed at answering a set of interrelated questions, which have emerged both in policy and academic circles, about China's role in this relatively new sphere. The most common question – which I have encountered and have myself been asked numerous times while carrying out research for this book – is: "Is China promoting an authoritarian version of the Internet in Africa?" This question, articulated in slightly different versions, has been more or less recurrent in popular debates. A relatively common variation has been: "Is China helping authoritarian regimes build their own Internets?" which resonates with criticism towards Chinese support of "rogue" states (e.g. Zimbabwe, Sudan, Eritrea) with whom most Western donors have severed ties or significantly disengaged. A less frequent but more pertinent question is: "Is China engaging in different ways with democratic and authoritarian states?" which slightly shifts the focus from China *doing something to* Africa, towards China *interacting with* existing institutional setups on the continent.

This book also seeks to answer questions that have been less often asked in China–Africa debates, but are essential to comprehensively understanding China's role as well as the future of information societies in Africa. One is: "How do the relative strength of the state, private companies, and civil society organizations in a given country influence the outcomes of projects developed in collaboration with the Chinese government or with Chinese companies?" This question problematizes the idea of "African agency" in China–Africa relations and interrogates how different actors within national borders have related to and been influenced by Chinese state and non-state entities.

I also seek to consider a limited set of forces that appear to have interacted with Chinese activities in the ICT sector, producing change in information societies across the continent. As mentioned above, one of these forces is the securitization of development and foreign policy, strongly supported by the United States. This aspect raises questions about whether China is strategically exploiting some of the contradictions of its adversaries, seeking to use them in order to more quietly assert its policies and visions.

All these questions presuppose a need to engage both with the political and technological components of China's entrance into Africa's ICT sector. And the answers I offer are informed by the need to overcome prevalent deterministic positions – which imply that technology developed in the "free world" will promote freedom and technology produced within the borders of an authoritarian regime will promote authoritarianism – and produce instead a deeper understanding of how different technologies, discourses, and actors interact in specific sociopolitical contexts, and what outcomes they actually produce.

In order to keep the technical and political together, the analysis of the evidence collected in Kenya, Ghana, Ethiopia, and Rwanda has been guided by a framework that marries insights from history of technology – to map how artifacts interact with different sociopolitical contexts and evolve over time – as well as from international relations and development studies – to understand how different actors and ideas compete for hegemony in a multipolar world. Centered on the concepts of *technopolitics* and *technopolitical regimes,* this framework aims to capture how national and international politics and technology shape one another, and how different balances of power influence the outcomes of innovation processes.

Applying such a framework to the study of China's role in Africa's ICT sector has both advantages and disadvantages. Having previously employed the concepts of technopolitics and technopolitical regimes to chart the unique history of conflict and innovation in Ethiopia,[24] I have learned how these tools are particularly powerful when a researcher is able to analyze a case in depth, to "plunge" into a technical artifact or assemblage, following the multiple cycles through which political ambitions interact with technological opportunities and constraints and evolve as a result of this interaction. Employing the same tools on a larger, comparative scale may reduce the ability to identify all the fractures and contradictions characterizing the evolution of a specific technological system. When is it that politics appears to prevail over technology, or vice versa? Why is this the case? And what outcomes do specific choices produce? At the same time, comparative analysis allows for the spotting of how large waves of innovation interact with local configurations of power and skills, understanding the nexus between the international and the national, and what elements can account for differences across nations.

In the specific case of China's involvement in African ICTs, the framework of technopolitics allows the disaggregating of elements that have tended to be bundled together in the study of China–Africa relations, often obscuring how each of them shapes key aspects in the evolution of national information societies. For example, it can account for how, while China has aggressively sought to push its technology into the continent, this effort has not been paralleled by an equal "discursive push" to present its model of the information society as more appealing or a better fit for Africa. Or, it encourages mapping the alliances created among different types of actors – identifying those who have been able to ride the wave created by a specific technology or those who have been weakened by an innovation they have not been able to master – to understand why a specific technopolitical regime took the shape it took.

Examining communication technologies through the lens of technopolitics involves the concurrent analysis of three inter-related components, which can each be studied as networks of similar elements: a network of *technologies*, a network of *discourses*, and a network of *actors*.

Network of technologies

The "same" technology can take on different shapes in different locations. Thomas Hughes employed the concept of style, used by art historians, to account for this phenomenon, registering and explaining technological variations observed across different cultural and political environments. In the case of electrification, for example, he explained how the distribution of power plants in London and Berlin differed for no particular technical reason, but responded to differences in the political and regulatory regimes of each country; conservative Britain, where private interests prevailed over the ability of central power to regulate the market, and socially democratic Germany, where the state took a greater role as a champion of electrification.[25] In the case of China and the Internet, it can be argued that it is a rudimentary understanding of this concept that led the US Congress to expect that large Chinese ICT companies (e.g. Huawei, ZTE) would try hiding back doors on their equipment in order to obtain sensitive information abroad, and thus adopted measures to prevent them from operating on US soil. It is, however, only a deeper, empirical engagement with technological artifacts – rather than assumptions based on preconceived ideas – that can allow an adequate understanding of how technology actually changes in a different context. This fuller, descriptive account of a specific configuration of technologies – a different style, to use Hughes' terminology – can then become an entry point to study more complex, often partially hidden, processes connecting politics and technology in a given location. In this particular case, leaks from the former US National Security Agency (NSA) contractor Edward Snowden later revealed that the NSA itself had tried to install secret elements within Huawei's equipment destined to be deployed in foreign countries, giving Congress's accusations an ironic twist.[26] As Thomas Rid succinctly put it, "there is now more publicly available evidence that the NSA exploited Huawei than there is public evidence that shows the PLA [Chinese People's Liberation Army] or other Chinese agencies did so."[27]

Network of discourses

The second element of the analysis involves the mapping of the discourses surrounding and informing a particular technology. As Pinch, Ashmore, and Mulkay have pointed out:

> Technologies are often made available through texts, and the meaning given to a technology through such texts can vary from context to context (and/or audience to audience) [...] It is only

by close attention to the different discursive contexts in which these definitions are offered and an examination of the rhetoric of technology that we can begin to understand the full richness of its multifaceted and interpretative nature.[28]

In the case of ICTs, new technologies, when proposed in countries that are likely to be adopters rather than innovators, often are not even visible. Only the potentials and expected uses described by the advocates of its application are. In this regard, China's behavior has differed from that exhibited by other technological exporters. As explained in Chapters 2 and 3, when companies such as Huawei or ZTE have proposed solutions to partners in Africa, they have indeed sought to explain the advantages and potentials of their technologies. However, in contrast to the US government or tech giants such as Facebook, neither the Chinese government nor Chinese companies have sought to produce macro-narratives about the Internet, proposing a supposed "Chinese model" ready for export.

Network of actors

A third element to take into consideration when examining the evolution of a specific form of technopolitics is the coalition of actors that emerges, or is created, around a technological artifact or assemblage. The relationship between a technology and the individuals, groups, and institutions embracing or opposing it is complex and constantly evolving. At the beginning of the global diffusion of the Internet, it was smaller and more adaptable organizations, such as start-ups and NGOs, that rode the wave of new technology to affirm new ideas and solutions. As Milton Mueller explained, "the explosion of ideas, services, and expression associated with the Internet's growth in the mid-1990s happened because states weren't prepared for it and because states weren't in charge."[29] Things have significantly changed since, and states have slowly, but decisively, learned how to use new technologies to affirm their own projects. China has played an important role in this process.

It is from the practical interaction of elements belonging to the three networks described above that a technopolitical regime progressively emerges. A technopolitical regime can thus be thought as the assemblage connecting nodes in each of these networks that are potentially further connected with other technologies, discourses, and actors. Once the links among these nodes are strengthened in ways that make each node part of a more cohesive whole, these nodes start to influence one another, or, more precisely, their more frequent and significant interactions are more likely to influence all nodes that are part of a technopolitical regime. Multiple regimes can emerge around the same technology and enter into competition with one another. It is power, in the end, that determines what regime is destined to prevail over its alternatives. As Allen and Hecht explained:

> Social choices shape technological development. But the resulting physical, financial, and institutional durability of systems means that, once developed, they – and the values they uphold – cannot be changed easily. As material manifestations of human choices, systems acquire momentum. In so doing they embody, reinforce, and enact social and political power. Thus, human power rides upon the history of things.[30]

In the case of China's rising role in African information societies, this conceptualization of technopolitics offers a means of understanding how, even if discursively China may have not clearly articulated its vision and position, the fact that it has supported specific technological solutions and entered into partnerships with specific types of actors may eventually influence the types of discourses that emerge and further shape the evolution of technology in a specific national context. Hence the importance of concurrently following changes across all three levels, registering whose visions have been turned into concrete policies or projects, and whose have been marginalized. In the case of this book, it has meant trying to collect the voices, ideas, and interpretations of a broad variety of actors, including African politicians – both in government and opposition – entrepreneurs, journalists, scholars, and activists, who have contributed to, or sought to contribute to, the evolution of the information society in their respective countries, as well as a constellation of external agents who sought to play a part in this evolution, including Chinese engineers and diplomats, American activists and journalists, international civil servants, and NGO workers. The material collected from interviews and other textual material (e.g. field notes, project documents) was then set alongside observations of how technical artifacts actually took shape, as part of an iterative process. Going "back and forth" between the technical and the discursive not only allowed capturing the conflicts emerging throughout the process of technological appropriation, but also uncovering how political actors were forced to reconsider their visions and ambitions as they interacted with technological possibilities and constraints.

A preliminary analysis: winners and losers

Analyzing China's influence on the shaping of information societies in Africa through the lenses of technopolitics meant tracing different, often overlapping, and sometimes contradictory trajectories. Depending on the level of analysis on which the research focused, different types of responses emerged, highlighting apparently conflicting aspects of China's role and impact, and different types of winners and losers.

At a *macro* level, the one mapping large, global trends, there are elements corroborating the image depicted at the beginning of this chapter, of different blocs competing to support alternative ideas of the Internet. Warnings of a new Cold War emerging over the Internet are exaggerated – countries are not being asked to pledge allegiance to one or another model and there is a great deal of hybridization and recombination happening on the ground – but two loose macro-regimes do appear to have emerged, one with the United States and the other with China at their center. As Ronald Deibert and his colleagues have pointed out, authoritarian regimes have progressively moved from the relatively simple tactic of blocking access to unwanted content and either rebuking or ignoring condemnation of this practice coming from the international community, to a more complex strategy of openly asserting the legitimacy of the measures they have adopted.[31] For China, the keyword of this strategy has been *sovereignty*, the reassertion of physical borders into the digital realm, allowing nations the freedom to choose their own conceptions of the Internet, based on cultural, social, and political factors. For some Internet scholars, the idea of redrawing borders online is not necessarily a bad one, and has proved a key element for providing targeted information to users, facilitating payments, and also ensuring communities can feel more rooted into norms that have guided them for much longer than the Internet has been around.[32] In addition, the idea of a sovereign Internet cannot be equated to the assertion or advocacy of any specific model. In principle, it simply aims at creating a space for national communities to decide how they want to build their own information society. The problem with this argument is that the Chinese government is not a scholar articulating a position on a given topic, but has massively intervened in ways that, as indicated by shifting the focus on other levels of analysis, can indeed have substantive implications and encourage changes in a specific direction.

At a *meso* level, the one focusing on groups and institutions, the establishment and reinforcement of cooperation on ICTs can be narrated as the rise of the capacity of the African state to shape information spaces. This aspect will be examined at length throughout the book, but can be presented here through the words of a Ghanaian technocrat reflecting on how the Chinese approach stood in contrast with the one employed by other development actors, and why, for him, it represented a better fit for the shaping of African information societies. As he argued, while explaining how his government sought funds to build a national fiber optic infrastructure:

> The idea was to support a backbone company owned by the government. We approached the EU and USAID, but there was a problem with the financing because they wanted the company owning the backbone to be private, while for us it had to be government owned. They did not understand that in Africa the government is the prime actor in development. Our idea was that a telecommunication infrastructure is like a highway. The EU and USAID would not come in if it was not private.

But for us the problem was that the private would not provide the social services. But the Chinese were ok. They accepted to support Ghana's broadband infrastructure facility to promote our information society. If you look at the WSIS declaration of principles, the commitment is to produce and create assets, distribute and consume to improve the living conditions of human kind. So those components were there. And the only way developing countries can participate in the information society is to build infrastructure. But the US is not committed to build infrastructure. But in Ghana we wanted an expensive state of the art backbone all over the country.[33]

The predilection of the state over other actors – NGOs, start-ups, incubators – to shape local information societies has emerged at the intersection of different strategies championed by China: the use of aid as a tool for foreign policy,[34] the preference of multi-lateralism over multi-stakeholderism as a framework for Internet governance, and China's own experience with a centrally directed emergence of the national information society. As discussed especially in Chapters 3 and 4, while this has allowed the state to boast its own plans, it has also led to the marginalization of other actors (e.g. activists, independent programmers, civil society organizations) in shaping the future of their national Internets.

At a *micro* level, the one focusing on individual users, the story of China–Africa and the Internet seems to contrast with the analysis at the other two levels, and depicts a bleaker picture for the future of the global Internet.

Anthropologist Miriam Driessen has offered a fascinating account of individual perceptions and self-perceptions of Chinese aid when examining infrastructural projects in rural Ethiopia. As she reported, Ethiopians living alongside the construction site where she conducted her fieldwork seemed not to appreciate the difference between "new" Chinese actors and previous agents of development. They often stole material owned by Chinese companies "to level their front or back yards," or to build "chapels and churches."[35] This appeared to infuriate Chinese managers and workers, and brought to light substantial contradictions between different conceptions of development. Similar to their Western counterparts, Chinese development actors adopted a high-modernist view of development as progressive and unilinear; they tended to ignore alternative, local ideas about development; and were prone to universalizing human motivation. As Driessen reported:

> Chinese managers attempt to fashion young Ethiopian men into diligent workers who submit themselves to management and to the higher cause of wealth accumulation. According to the Chinese viewpoint, these workers care more about religion (or what the Chinese migrants referred to as "Jesus") than about money. The Ethiopians steal rather than struggle to make a living for themselves, as one Chinese accountant put it, and as a result are labelled as lazy. Once again, the colonial trope of the indolent native is repeated. What the Chinese see as a novel and fairer form of development assistance in Africa actually shares many characteristics with the old, and arguably superseded, Western approach to delivering "aid."[36]

Similarly, when examined from the perspective of individual users, China's entrance into Africa's ICT sector may ultimately not appear too different from the experience accumulated with Western donors, despite claims to the contrary. Dominant narratives on China's role in shaping the global Internet have stressed its distinctive stance and disruptive potential – either when spun by Western competitors presenting China as leading a coalition of authoritarian states embracing a more closed version of the Internet, or by China itself, emphasizing its support for the sovereign right of states, especially in the Global South, to shape their national information societies.

When analyzed more carefully, however, some key decisions shaping the technical and political architecture of the Internet have shown a more pragmatic – and less ideological – tendency of actors from the East and from the West to align and cooperate when this meant increasing their ability to surveil and control users, either for political or commercial gains, or for both. As will be discussed in Chapter 5, when examining the position of different countries with regard to the standardization of deep packet inspection – a data-processing technique allowing big players, state or corporate, to read the content of online communications in real time – representatives from China, the United States, and most other countries participating in the event were swift in passing a measure that in practice "normalized" the adoption of a technology eroding key principles on which the Internet was built, especially the right of users to not be discriminated against for what they communicate and receive over the network.[37]

From this perspective, the projects and practices supported by the Chinese government or by Chinese companies in Africa appear neither more malevolent nor more benevolent than those of their competitors and adversaries. Similar to what large corporate players (e.g. Google, Facebook) are doing, they go in the direction of expanding access and services, at the expense of making users more legible, surveilled, and controlled. China's actions thus simply appear to be contributing to – rather than having created – a trend that has progressively eroded the possibilities of shaping the Internet from below and has concentrated the power into the hands of fewer and fewer corporate and public agents. Similar to the case illustrated by Driessen, individuals may still be offered opportunities to disrupt some elements of these trajectories decided from above, by asserting different values and a different conception of development, but are given very little chance to change those trajectories altogether.

Plan of the book

The book progresses by analyzing different aspects of China's involvement in Africa's ICT sector, connecting it with broader processes that have shaped the unique trajectories of information societies in Ethiopia, Rwanda, Kenya, and Ghana, as well as with global trends in Internet governance and development.

Chapter 2 begins by exploring the motivations and modes that have informed Chinese engagement into Africa's ICT sector, while Chapter 3 analyzes some of the emerging trends on the ground, by comparing how two democracies – Kenya and Ghana – and two autocracies – Ethiopia and Rwanda – have related to Chinese support and ideas. Chapter 4 further examines how China and its information society are perceived in Africa, posing questions on the appeal of the strategies developed by the Chinese regime for different types of actors in Africa. Chapter 5 shifts the focus on other processes of international relevance and scale that have influenced the shaping of information societies in Africa, asking whether and how they have interacted with projects and visions promoted by China. Chapter 6 concludes by reinstating some of the main, empirically grounded, arguments made throughout the book and advancing some possible alternative interpretations.

Notes

1 Bill Clinton, "Full Text of Clinton's Speech on China Trade Bill," *The New York Times*, March 9, 2000, https://partners.nytimes.com/library/world/asia/030900clinton-china-text.html?mcubz=0.

2 Hillary Clinton, "Remarks on Internet Freedom," *US Department of State*, January 21, 2010, www.state.gov/secretary/rm/2010/01/135519.htm.

3 Alexander Klimburg, "The Internet Yalta," *Center for a New American Security*, 2013, 2.

4 Frank Webster, *Theories of the Information Society* (Routledge, 2014), 8.

5 Matthew Hindman, *The Myth of Digital Democracy* (Princeton University Press, 2008); Robert J. Gordon, *The Rise and Fall of American Growth: The US Standard of Living since the Civil War*, vol. 70 (Princeton University Press, 2017).

6 Sarah Cook, "The Long Shadow of Chinese Censorship," 2013, http://ignucius.bd.ub.es:8180/jspui/handle/123456789/787; Douglas Farah and Andy Mosher, *Winds from the East* (Center for International Media Assistance, 2010).

7 Eric Schmidt and Jared Cohen, *The New Digital Age: Reshaping the Future of People, Nations and Business* (Random House, 2013).

8 Hamza Shaban, "Former Google Chief Predicts the Internet Will Split by 2028: A Chinese Web and an American One," *Washington Post*, 2018, www.washingtonpost.com/technology/2018/09/21/former-google-chief-predicts-internet-will-split-by-chinese-web-an-american-one/.

9 Farah and Mosher, *Winds from the East*.

10 Joshua Kurlantzick, *Charm Offensive: How China's Soft Power Is Transforming the World* (Yale University Press, 2007).

11 For a systematic review of the difference within and beyond Western media systems, see Daniel Hallin and Paolo Mancini, *Comparing Media Systems : Three Models of Media and Politics* (Cambridge University Press, 2004); Daniel C. Hallin and Paolo Mancini, *Comparing Media Systems beyond the Western World* (Cambridge University Press, 2011).

12 Tim Allen and Nicole Stremlau, "Media Policy, Peace and State Reconstruction," 2005, 5, http://eprints.lse.ac.uk/28347.

13 Allen and Stremlau, "Media Policy," 5.

14 Many of these studies will be discussed throughout the book, but for a quick snapshot, see, for example, Zhang Yanqiu and Simon Matingwina, "Constructive Journalism: A New Journalistic Paradigm of Chinese Media in Africa," in *China's Media and Soft Power in Africa*, Palgrave Series in Asia and Pacific Studies (Palgrave Macmillan, 2016), 93–105; Bob Wekesa, "Emerging Trends and Patterns in China–Africa Media Dynamics: A Discussion from an East African Perspective," *Ecquid Novi: African Journalism Studies* 34, no. 3 (2013): 62–78; Emeka Umejei, "Hybridizing Journalism: Clash of Two 'Journalisms' in Africa," *Chinese Journal of Communication*, May 18, 2018, 1–15; Dani Madrid-Morales and Herman Wasserman, "Chinese Media Engagement in South Africa: What Is Its Impact on Local Journalism?" *Journalism Studies*, 2017, 1–18; Vivien Marsh, "Mixed Messages, Partial Pictures? Discourses under Construction in CCTV's Africa Live Compared with the BBC," *Chinese Journal of Communication* 9, no. 1 (2016): 56–70.

15 See, for example Klimburg, "The Internet Yalta."

16 Cook, "The Long Shadow of Chinese Censorship."

17 See, for example, Giles Mohan and Ben Lampert, "Negotiating China: Reinserting African Agency into China–Africa Relations," *African Affairs* 112, no. 446 (2013): 92–110; Pádraig Carmody and Ian Taylor, "Flexigemony and Force in China's Resource Diplomacy in Africa: Sudan and Zambia Compared," *Geopolitics* 15, no. 3 (2010): 496–515.

18 Aleksandra W. Gadzala, *Africa and China: How Africans and Their Governments Are Shaping Relations with China* (Rowman & Littlefield, 2015).

19 Joan Tilouine and Ghalia Kadiri, "A Addis-Abeba, le siège de l'Union africaine espionné par Pékin," *Le Monde*, January 26, 2018, www.lemonde.fr/afrique/article/2018/01/26/a-addis-abeba-le-siege-de-l-union-africaine-espionne-par-les-chinois_5247521_3212.html.

20 There is a long history of American and European heads of state and ministers warning about China's nefarious influence on the continent during their visits to Africa. US Secretary of State Hillary Clinton, in her 2011 trip to Dar El Salaam, warned about the risk of "new colonialism" in Africa. UK Prime Minister David Cameron similarly mentioned during a speech in Lagos the same year that China may export its "authoritarian capitalism." Flavia Krause-Jackson, "Clinton Chastises China on Internet, African 'New Colonialism,'" *Bloomberg*, June 11, 2011, www.bloomberg.com/news/articles/2011-06-11/

clinton-chastises-china-on-internet-african-new-colonialism-; Jason Groves, "Cameron Warns Africans over the 'Chinese Invasion' as They Pour Billions into Continent," *Daily Mail*, July 19, 2011, www.dailymail.co.uk/news/article-2016677/Cameron-warns-Africans-Chinese-invasion-pour-billions-continent.html.

21 Aaron Maasho, "China Denies Report It Hacked African Union Headquarters," *Reuters*, January 29, 2018, www.reuters.com/article/us-africanunion-summit-china/china-denies-report-it-hacked-african-union-headquarters-idUSKBN1FI2I5. Kagame, at the same time, took this as an opportunity to reassert his view it was shameful African leaders had to rely on Chinese benevolence to have their headquarters revamped. As he made clear, "I would only have wished that in Africa we had got our act together earlier on. We should have been able to build our own building."

22 Eric Olander, "Why China Is Pushing Back So Hard against Spying Accusations in Africa," February 17, 2018, www.youtube.com/watch?v=ntwa9iKJ85M.

23 Kabweza, "Chinese Style Internet Censorship Coming to Zimbabwe – President Mugabe," *Techzim*, April 4, 2016, www.techzim.co.zw/2016/04/china-style-internet-censorship-coming-to-zimbabwe-president-mugabe/. Zimbabwe's former President Robert Mugabe was the only head of state to openly declare the need to adopt measures of the kind developed in China to control and shape the Internet in Africa.

24 Iginio Gagliardone, *The Politics of Technology in Africa* (Cambridge University Press, 2016).

25 Thomas P. Hughes, *Networks of Power: Electrification in Western Society, 1880–1930* (Johns Hopkins University Press, 1983).

26 Glenn Greenwald, *No Place to Hide* (Penguin, 2014).

27 Thomas Rid, "Snowden, 多谢 多谢 | Kings of War," 2014, http://kingsofwar.org.uk/2014/03/snowden-thanks-very-much/.

28 Trevor J. Pinch, Malcolm Ashmore, and Michael Mulkay, "Technology, Testing, Text: Clinical Budgeting in the UK National Health Service," in *Shaping Technology/Building Society. Studies in Sociotechnical Change*, ed. Wiebe E. Bijker and John Law (MIT Press, 1992), 242.

29 Milton Mueller, *Network and States: The Global Politics of Internet Governance* (MIT Press, 2010), 185.

30 Michael Allen and Gabrielle Hecht, *Technologies of Power : Essays in Honor of Thomas Parke Hughes and Agatha Chipley Hughes* (MIT Press, 2001), 2–3.

31 Ronald Deibert et al., *Access Denied: The Practice and Policy of Global Internet Filtering* (MIT Press, 2008); Ronald Deibert et al., *Access Controlled: The Shaping of Power, Rights, and Rule in Cyberspace* (MIT Press, 2010); Ronald

Deibert et al., *Access Contested: Security, Identity, and Resistance in Asian Cyberspace* (MIT Press, 2012).

32 Jack L. Goldsmith and Tim Wu, *Who Controls the Internet? Illusions of a Borderless World* (Oxford University Press, 2006), http://jost.syr.edu/wp-content/uploads/who-controls-the-internet_illusions-of-a-borderless-world.pdf.

33 Interview: Issah Yahaya, Director of Policy Planning in the Ministry of Communication. Accra, Ghana, August 19, 2010.

34 Carmody and Taylor, "Flexigemony and Force in China's Resource Diplomacy in Africa"; Johan Lagerkvist, "Chinese Eyes on Africa: Authoritarian Flexibility versus Democratic Governance," *Journal of Contemporary African Studies* 27, no. 2 (2009): 119–134.

35 Miriam Driessen, "The African Bill: Chinese Struggles with Development Assistance," *Anthropology Today* 31, no. 1 (2015): 6.

36 Driessen, "The African Bill," 7.

37 Ralf Bendrath and Milton Mueller, "The End of the Net as We Know It? Deep Packet Inspection and Internet Governance," *New Media & Society* 13, no. 7 (November 1, 2011): 1142–1160, https://doi.org/10.1177/1461444811398031; Glyn Moody, "ITU Approves Deep Packet Inspection Standard Behind Closed Doors, Ignores Huge Privacy Implications," *Techdirt*, 2012, www.techdirt.com/articles/20121203/07493221209/itu-approves-deep-packet-inspection-standard-behind-closed-doors-ignores-huge-privacy-implications.shtml.

2 | CHINA AS PARTNER

Financing Africa's information societies

On May 13, 2007, NigComSat-1, Africa's first communication satellite, was launched aboard a *Long March* rocket at the Xichang Space Center, in southwest China.[1] Envisaged by Nigeria's National Space Research and Development Agency, but built in and operated from China, the satellite was meant to mark the beginning of a new era for both countries. For Nigeria, it was a visible assertion of its willingness to invest in ICTs and take a leadership role in Africa. The launch was publicly framed as the pinnacle of Nigeria's commitment towards building an "information-based economy," reducing the digital divide, and offering new types of services, from distance learning to access to government records.[2] China, with NigComSat-1, sent a signal to the world that it had become a credible alternative in the commercial space race, especially for countries with fewer resources.[3] The cooperation with Nigeria's space program was the first opportunity to showcase China's ability to assist another country in the complex process going from the envisioning of a satellite, to its construction and launch into space.[4]

This experience displays some essential features that have come to characterize China–Africa relations in the communication sector more broadly.

China has demonstrated its readiness to invest in areas deemed by foreign investors and donors as too risky, not sufficiently profitable, or not high priorities in the aid agenda. China not only provided the expertise to build, launch, and operate NigComSat-1, but also granted US$200 million worth of preferential buyer credits to Nigeria, covering two-thirds of the total cost of the project.[5] This generosity, however, did not come without trade-offs. China acquired the opportunity to experiment in a relatively new area, but this had repercussions on the quality of service, at least in the initial phases. Eighteen months after its launch, NigComSat-1 ran out of power because of a malfunction with its solar array and was later decommissioned. Nigerians had to wait until December 2011 to see a replacement satellite regain the orbit and resume operations.[6]

Another feature of China's support in the expansion of the ICT sector in Africa has been its ability to fit into each country's distinct development trajectory, rather than following template approaches. Nigeria has occupied a unique place in Africa for its determination to invest in satellite technology, not only for communications, but also to oversee oilfields, control pollution, and monitor elections.[7] Differently from other donor countries, China spent little time reminding its Nigerian partners about their development priorities, and that investments in such an expensive sector might clash with commitments to reduce poverty. On the contrary, the Chinese government and the Chinese companies involved in the project seized this as an opportunity to reinforce the image of China supporting developing countries in their distinctive paths towards development.

The launch of NigComSat-1 also offers a glimpse of Africa's role in China's broader strategy of engagement with countries that are further away from its immediate sphere of influence. As this book illustrates by analyzing cases related to the shaping of Africa's information societies, Chinese political and economic actors have often looked at Africa as a space to gain experience, test ideas, and fill in the gaps left by other international actors, all while keeping an eye on how these experiences could eventually turn useful on other terrains. Many African politicians, entrepreneurs, and activists I interviewed shared the feeling that current Chinese initiatives in Africa seemed to be pieces of a grander strategy whose contours were still too difficult to clearly discern. Delving too much into these ideas may be problematic, as conspiratorial tones related to China's expansion overseas already abound. However, looking at past experiences, it is instructive to notice how a similar strategy, which evokes Chairman Mao's famous exhortation of encircling the cities from the countryside, has supported some of China's most successful ICT companies. It was through winning contracts where larger companies had little interest to venture, and investing significantly in research and development (R&D) in ways that could allow customization and fast learning from previous experiences, that Huawei progressively became one of China's leading multinational corporations. A similar strategy is being now applied to its expansion into Africa.

The next sections address these phenomena with greater detail and focus. They first examine the drivers of China's expansion in the ICT sector in Africa, and then turn to the analysis of the strategies adopted by the Chinese government and by Chinese companies to invest and support ICTs across the continent, and how they compare with those followed by traditional Western donors.

Why is China investing in Africa's ICTs?

China's investment in communication technologies is one of the latest stages in the history of its engagement with Africa. China now hosts the largest population of Internet users in the world,[8] and Huawei is the world's largest telecommunication equipment maker,[9] but China's own experience with the Internet and other new communication technologies is relatively recent and relied heavily on foreign investment and expertise in the initial phases. The key traits of China's information society and its evolution will be discussed later in the book, but it is important to remark how the expansion in Africa does not represent a separate chapter in the history of this evolution. Similar to the establishment of stronger relations with African countries to access raw materials needed for the growth of the Chinese economy, investments in the communication sector in foreign countries are a constitutive component in the process of growth of China's information economy, both at the material and ideational level.

China's expansion in Africa's ICT sector has been rapid, but not necessarily linear, and has variously connected large public companies, resellers of affordable tech products, emerging software multinationals, and a skilled workforce seeking a better fortune abroad. These actors have pursued different goals and have contributed to create often-contradictory images of China's role in Africa's information societies, but they have all been somehow influenced by three interrelated processes. The first is the launch of China's "Go Out" strategy, unveiled in 1999 and later incorporated into the 10th Five-Year Plan (2001–2005) with the objective of encouraging Chinese enterprises to invest overseas, improve competitiveness, and secure an international business presence. The second is China's quest to strengthen its soft power, shaping African, and global, public opinion in its favor. This goal has been directly pursued through the launch of large media initiatives in Africa, but has also had an impact on ordinary Chinese expatriates, whose behavior in Africa has been placed under scrutiny. Finally, China's own Africa policy has increasingly emphasized diversifying interventions on the continent, venturing in new sectors. Media and telecommunications have been one of the key elements in this process of expansion.

"Go Out"

China's "Go Out" strategy has been traced back to numerous factors, from China's surplus of savings, to the need to secure natural resources, to its interest in strengthening its "comprehensive national power".[10] In the case of ICTs, this policy came into force at a crucial time in the evolution of China's domestic market. After a decade of fierce competition, two companies, Huawei and ZTE, had emerged among the most successful in a fast-evolving sector. Huawei was founded in 1987 by a former lieutenant of the People's Liberation Army, Ren Zhengfei. It began manufacturing phone switches, later expanding its offer to building telecommunication networks and developing products for the consumer market. Zhongxing New Telecommunications Equipment (ZTE) was created in 1985 as an offspring of China's Ministry of Aerospace, but was later publicly listed in Shenzhen and Hong Kong.

Despite having to compete with numerous other companies, some with stronger backing from the Chinese government (e.g. Great Dragon, Putian, Datang), Huawei and ZTE steadily rose to prominence, and by the early 2000s had graduated as two of the country's most successful multinational telecommunication corporations. Some argue it was precisely their relative independence from government interference, together with strong investments in R&D, that underpinned the companies' success.[11] But once they had emerged from a crowded market, Huawei and ZTE certainly became the two national champions on which the government bet for venturing out in foreign markets. In Africa, almost all contracts signed in telecommunications saw an involvement of either Huawei or ZTE, and often both companies competed for the shares of a project or the local market.

Part of Huawei's success in China depended on its ability to tap into unexploited and relatively peripheral markets and grow stronger from there. A similar strategy has been adopted overseas, and it has proven successful when followed closely. When Huawei ventured into highly competitive markets, including Europe and North America, it encountered strong resistance and was ultimately forced to backtrack. Alleged collusion with the Chinese government and Ren's links with the army were used in the United States, Australia, and later in the United Kingdom as motives to oppose or reconsider Huawei's presence in their respective national markets because of concern of breaches in security.[12] In Africa, on the contrary, Huawei, and the same argument can be extended to ZTE and other Chinese companies, has found a much easier terrain to grow and experiment.

The African entrepreneurs, experts, and engineers I interviewed seemed fully aware that Chinese companies were not just acting as benevolent partners, but were using contracts in Africa to gain experience and expand their reach. As an Ethiopian entrepreneur commented, referring to the large contract ZTE had secured with her government: "We are cheap R&D for them. They want to get experience and market share."[13] Another Ethiopian expert, who had been closely working with the country's only telecom operator, further explained:

They are sending junior engineers here. They do everything
by calling their R&D engineers back in Beijing. So you do not
get the answers locally and according to what is needed on
the ground, but directly from China. And they do not transfer
knowledge. Many of the engineers are here just for three
months on a visitor visa and then they come back. Some others
stay for a bit longer and they provide support. They see us as a
learning school.[14]

This perspective seemed to be shared by experts across the continent, recognizing the unique ability of Chinese companies to
mobilize vast resources, but also a relative lack of sophistication.
As a young Ghanaian entrepreneur explained:

They approach the business holistically. But the problem is that
if one specific product is mature and works well, others are not,
but they are still part of the package. Their strategy is to keep
working on it and fixing it until it works fine. But there must
be a balance between quality and responsiveness. They throw
many things hoping that one will stick. They flood the market
with products and services hoping that some will pick up. Our
strategy instead is more about focus.[15]

Among tech elites, however, this strategy has been generally perceived more as an unavoidable component of China's growing
exposure in Africa, rather than a reason for resentment. In some
instances, the tendency of Chinese companies to learn through
trial and error has been perceived on the contrary as a good fit
for Africa's emerging telecommunications sector. As a Kenyan
entrepreneur commented: "The Chinese are more willing to cus-
tomize. So it is not only the traditional sector, it is not just selling
equipment and phones, they are working with every operator to
support their networks".[16]

This predisposition to interpret Africa as a learning ground
where Chinese companies, citizens, and institutions can find
their feet and learn to compete in a foreign environment is not
unique to the ICT sector. As other scholars who have examined
the encounter between Chinese and Africans have explained,

it is the expression of a complex mix of feelings, including self-perceptions of superiority as well as inferiority, and is animated by an inescapable drive towards new opportunities. As Howard French has reported through the words of a Chinese entrepreneur in Mozambique:

> Can you imagine if I had gone to America or to Germany first? The people in those places are too smart. I wouldn't have gotten anywhere. I don't think I could have beaten them. So we had to find backward countries, poor countries that we can lead, places where we can do business, where we can manage things successfully.[17]

This testimony also accounts for the significant differences between official rhetoric, spinning ideas of mutual benefit and learning, and lived experiences, shaped by unavoidable tensions between competing interests and desires of domination. While these tensions have been most common in the case of relatively small Chinese businesses, some of the largest Chinese multinational corporations – Huawei above all – have sought ways to fight back, counteracting narratives framing Chinese companies as exploitative and unwilling to transfer knowledge. Learning academies have been opened in African universities. Initiatives such as Huawei's "Seeds for the Future" have been selecting some of the brightest students with an interest in ICTs and have offered them opportunities for receiving training in China.[18] As a Huawei employee in Kenya explained:

> We have a corporate social responsibility program. Huawei is the only Chinese company doing CSR in Africa. We support students. But in general the Chinese government supports the idea of companies doing CSR. And 14% of our budget goes into R&D. We have partnerships with a number of universities to support their students and we have also opened a lab at Strathmore University. We created a HANA [Huawei Authorized Networking Academy] that can offer certifications. With Moi University we collaborated on a curriculum review. And some students came as interns to work with Huawei.[19]

Programs such as "Seed for the Future," allowing selected graduates to visit and undergo training in China for a period from just two to four weeks, have been called into question as real contributions to knowledge transfer.[20] However, the evolution from an exclusive emphasis on turnkey projects to broader interventions, including partnerships with local training and academic institutions and efforts in shaping how projects in foreign markets are interpreted, represents an additional indication of the ability of Chinese companies to take cues from their competitors and use them to improve their own standing in emerging markets.

Hardware and soft power

China's soft power has become the subject of an increasing body of literature, exploring the differences that may exist between conceptions of soft power in China and in the United States, and analyzing some of the projects that have been actually realized to boost China's image abroad.[21]

Chinese scholars have focused on foundational questions such as "What is [soft power]? Does China have it? Where can China find it? Can it be bought? What should China do with it?"[22] Outside of China, a large share of the attention has been captured by the outcomes of China's reinvigorated interest in shaping its image abroad, including the proliferation of Confucius Institutes, or the expansion of Chinese media internationally at a time when most media companies headquartered in the United States and in Europe are pulling correspondents out of Africa. I have offered my contribution to this debate elsewhere, illustrating, for example, the strategies pursued by the African arm of Chinese broadcaster China Central Television (CCTV) – later rebranded China Global Television Network (CGTN) – to present a new narrative for both China and Africa, as well as the realities of African and Chinese journalists seeking a difficult balance between national interests and a type of journalism that can win audiences across the continent.[23] This book's emphasis on competing conceptions of the Internet and of the information society, however, encourages focusing on another, probably less apparent, aspect of China's projection of its image abroad.

New communication technologies, when considered as material artifacts – from the increasingly ubiquitous mobile phones to the fiber optic cables, routers, and servers needed for them to operate, but invisible to most – can reveal some significant contradictions, and recent innovations, in China's relationship with Africa.

China's distinctive approach to development, which has emphasized big infrastructural projects over less visible investments – for example, in governance or education – championed by other donors, has received praise and ensured many people in Africa are aware of China's support. As an Ethiopian scholar simply put it, "China is visible. If you ask people on the street what the U.S. have done here they would not know. But if you ask them about China, I am sure they will tell you something."[24] Before the massive expansion of Chinese media in Africa seeking to influence local public opinion, it was these large-scale infrastructural projects that symbolized – and continue to symbolize –China's efforts in the continent for a mass audience.

These efforts seem to have produced significant results, especially at the grassroots level. As the Afrobarometer's latest wave of surveys in Africa indicated, China's investment in infrastructure is by far the most important factor contributing to a positive image of China. Across the 35 countries surveyed, 32% of respondents placed infrastructural support on top, followed by the cost of Chinese products (23%) and China's business investment (16%).[25]

Also, in the case of ICTs, China's largest contribution has been in infrastructure – as compared, for example, to training or support to e-government or e-education preferred by other donors.

Information infrastructures, however, seem to be caught in a paradox. Similar to roads and dams, they require massive investments. Differently from them, they remain rather invisible. While the Chinese government has placed great emphasis on large infrastructural projects – especially roads and dams – and benefited from their ability to display China's might and friendship to wide audiences, when it comes to communication infrastructures this potential seems to vanish. There are other ways, however, to examine this paradox.

Invisibility in the ICT sector may not appear too bad after all, especially when considered in the context of the negative reputation Chinese products have acquired on the consumer market, as inexpensive but often unreliable. The same Afrobarometer survey that placed investments in infrastructure at the top for supporting positive attitudes towards China revealed that the quality of Chinese products is the most significant factor shaping negative perceptions (35%), followed by taking jobs or business from local actors (14%) and the extraction of resources from Africa (10%).[26]

As a marketing manager of StarTimes, a Chinese company that has aggressively entered the market of digital television in Africa, explained:

We need to transform the perception that many people have of Chinese products as low-quality products. A lot of people when they think about getting the decoder may ask: "Will it work?" For a long time, the Chinese products represented the cheaper option. If you go downtown you can always see Chinese phones that are much cheaper. So, we have to be aware of that. In our marketing strategy we do not present ourselves as a Chinese company, but as a Pan-African company. We are not a Chinese brand, even if when there is an article about us in the papers they refer to us as a Chinese company, which is ok. But in the ads we avoid any association with China.[27]

Beyond largely positive attitudes towards megaprojects and negative ones towards cheap consumer products, yet another perspective from which to look at China's growing presence in Africa's ICT sector has recently become increasingly relevant. Communication technologies have progressively emerged as an emblem of China's transformation, from a source of cheap goods appealing to those who could not afford better products, to a powerhouse able to compete in different segments of the market, including the most innovative ones. This process is relevant in Africa, but also globally; it is impacting the consumer market – where high-end phones branded Huawei and Xiaomi have gained stronger reputation and shares – but also niches where China has sought to counteract deep-rooted perceptions and stereotypes.

As a Ghanaian engineer engaged in digital migration reported after a visit to China:

> Before going to China I thought they were not very advanced. The image we have here of Chinese products in general is that they are not of very good quality. But during my trip I realized that they are doing very well. In the past we were thinking of just going to the West for those kind of deals, but China has become a strong competitor.[28]

In my own visits to Huawei's headquarters in Shenzhen, it was impressive to notice how entire floors of the company's main buildings had become exhibition centers where guided tours were offered to Chinese and foreign visitors, displaying the company's latest innovations in R&D-intensive sectors such as 5G connectivity and the Internet of things. This approach is shared by many other hi-tech businesses in Shenzhen, including Tencent, China's largest social networking and gaming firm, and DJI, the world leader in the civilian drone industry, which created spaces and opportunities to display their recent history, underling the rapid rise from humble beginnings to global leadership.

For African and foreign publics in general, this progressive transformation may be subtler than other aspects of China's soft power that have attracted attention to date – from the opening of Confucius Institutes, to the expansion of state media, to official visits – but can have long-lasting effects. It testifies of China's ability to rise and compete, to lead by example, in an increasingly crowded space where many actors are trying to secure their positions. It also encourages looking beyond the framework of China's assistance to Africa, and exploring how relationships of a commercial nature can influence the perceptions of China on the continent.

China's Africa policy and its diversification

A third process that has contributed to the increasing Chinese involvement in the ICT sector is the progressive diversification of China's own Africa policy.

Despite the reinvigorated relations between China and Africa having received significant attention in the popular press, in policy circles, and academia, Africa has scored as a comparatively low priority in China's overall foreign policy agenda.[29] As foreign affairs analyst Yun Sun stressed, Africa's importance:

> is mostly as a means to China's political and economic ends. Africa in general is excluded from the "strategically important" category and does not reach the highest level of decision making. Most Africa policies are procedural decisions made under existing guidelines.[30]

This description fits with the emphasis placed on the initial phases of China's re-engagement with Africa on two large-scale and inter-related factors as drivers of China–Africa relations: securing natural resources and seeking new markets for its manufactured goods.

While raw materials and consumer products continue to represent the pillars of China's presence in Africa, in the past few years the Chinese government has sought to add new elements to redefine this relation. FOCAC's third meeting in Beijing in 2006 represented a turning point in this respect. In the context of growing pledges in a variety of sectors, including collaborations in solar energy, medicine, and aviation, ICTs gained unprecedented attention. As FOCAC's Plan of Action reported:

> The two sides agreed to strengthen cooperation in information infrastructure building, IT application, general telecommunications services, cyber and information security, and telecommunications human resources development. China supports the African countries in their efforts to narrow the digital divide and accelerate the building of an information society based on the proposals of the World Summit on the Information Society held in Tunisia.[31]

While some projects had been realized in previous years – from joint ventures to create Sino-African telecom operators in the DRC to network expansion projects in Burundi – 2006 represented a watershed moment, marking a rapid spike in the number of ICT initiatives in Africa. New agreements were signed between the Chinese government and its African counterparts, going from supporting the laying of a fiber optic submarine cable in the Comoros, to the upgrade of the fixed and mobile infrastructures in Eritrea and Zimbabwe, to the provision of training and industrial equipment in Lesotho. This trend was not simply a temporary outcome of the grandiosity the Chinese government sought to display during FOCAC in 2006, but continued well into the following years, with new agreements signed in Angola, Sierra Leone, and Guinea-Bissau, and older projects extended or expanded in countries where Chinese companies had already marked their presence, such as Egypt or the DRC.

The sixth FOCAC meeting, which took place in South Africa in 2015, further consolidated the trend towards diversification. China's second Africa Policy Paper, released during the event – almost ten years after the first Policy Paper was launched in 2006 – displayed efforts to further expand and systematize areas of cooperation between China and Africa and to add new keywords – including the principles of "sincerity, practical results, affinity and good faith" – to inform the relationship between Chinese and African counterparts.[32]

While it is still unclear how these attempts to reword China–Africa relations will have practical repercussions, whether they are just spin or are reflective of deeper transformations, one area included in the Policy Paper, party-to-party relationships, seems to have received a significant boost already.

In 2017, the ruling parties of Ethiopia and Tanzania, the Ethiopian People's Revolutionary Democratic Front (EPRDF) and the Chama Cha Mapinduzi (CCM), both with strong socialist roots, have declared their plans to further strengthen their relationship with the Communist Party of China (CPC).[33] As a Tanzanian columnist writing for the *China Daily* stressed:

> Contrary to Western propaganda, the Chinese listen to minority voices, but have only a single national political party in place. [...] CCM should revert to Socialism (Ujamaa) as a rational choice. It should draw social-economic programmes that augur well for the have-nots.[34]

To date, the apparent re-ideologization of China–Africa relations does not seem to have led to developing a shared, publicly available vision of how information should fare in socialist countries, but, as indicated later in the book, exchanges among key political figures in countries such as Ethiopia have resulted in appreciation of the path followed by the CPC to shape its relationship with Chinese citizens.

Financing ICTs: aid, investment, or just something else?

Cutting across the three processes described above is a question about the means adopted to support China's expansion in Africa's ICT sector. While initial efforts to sponsor ICT projects in Africa were clearly tied to bilateral accords between governments in the framework of development cooperation, the rapid expansion of China's domestic ICT sector, improved competitiveness of Chinese firms, and their global exposure has made distinguishing Chinese support to ICT projects as aid, investment, or part of purely commercial relationships increasingly difficult.

To make things more complicated, the Chinese government, even when providing assistance as part of a relationship that can be identified as one between a donor and a recipient, has set itself apart from other donors in ways that defy attempts to box its interventions in predefined categories. As I have sought to explain elsewhere,[35] unpacking the specific strategies used by China to support ICTs in Africa, and how they compare to the strategies championed by "traditional" Western donors, requires engaging with at least two major debates, which are far from being settled and have been little aware of one another.

The first debate revolves around what should and should not be considered media development. This debate has been animated by scholars,[36] donors, international organizations (e.g. USAID, IDRC, UNESCO), NGOs, and foundations (e.g. Internews, IREX, BBC Media Action, the National Endowment for Democracy, the Knight, Ford, and Gates Foundations). As surveys of donor agencies supporting media development have indicated,[37] most donors seem to have developed a paradoxical relationship with the media and with communication technologies. Many agencies recognize the role of strong and unfettered media, and the importance of investing in projects harnessing the power of ICTs, but are frustrated by the inability of monitoring and evaluating the effects that investments in this area are producing. Scholars, for their part, have advanced different, but often overlapping, categorizations of media development,[38] and have called for "problematizing" and updating the whole concept.[39] The rising complexity characterizing media ecologies, along with the emergence of new platforms for expression, including social media, has made understanding which media should be most effectively targeted through assistance increasingly difficult.[40]

Despite the differences and ongoing contentions, however, the analysis of both practical and conceptual approaches to media development indicates that at least three overarching modes of operation have tended to characterize most interventions in this area: the building of a regulatory and legal framework; the supporting of infrastructure and capital equipment; and training and capacity-building.[41] I thus consider these three dimensions when analyzing China's approach.

The second, larger, debate that should be taken into consideration when seeking to understand China's entrance as a major player in the media and telecommunications sectors in Africa is on the very nature of aid and the standards that should be applied to distinguish it from other financial flows from richer to poorer countries. Different from the definition of media development, in this case "traditional" donor agencies have sought to reach consensus on common criteria. The 24 members of the Development Assistance Committee (DAC) recognize as Official Development Assistance (ODA) all:

> flows of official financing administered with the promotion of the economic development and welfare of developing countries as the main objective and which are concessional in character with a grant element of at least 25 per cent (using a fixed 10 per cent rate of discount) ... Lending by export credit agencies – with the pure purpose of export promotion – is excluded.[42]

As Deborah Brautigam has pointed out, however, this definition is not without problems.[43] In some cases, loans can be registered as aid even if the interest rate charged is much higher than what is normally charged by private banks. Also, when the DAC settled on a definition of ODA, it also defined a residual category of "other official flows" (OOF) as resources coming from governments but failing to meet the ODA criteria. While ample scholarship is available on ODA,[44] its disbursement, and effects, very little research has been conducted on OOF and their potential developmental outcomes, their ability to produce "economic development and welfare," even if it does not comply with the technical definition of aid.[45]

China's unprecedented engagement in developing countries and its increased activity in the ICT sector represent a challenge for both debates.

In contrast to donors stressing their determination to push other countries' media systems towards greater openness, China has distinguished itself for providing support with no strings attached, refraining from imposing a particular policy agenda as part of a cooperation package, and collaborating with democracies and autocracies alike – even if its relation with rogue states has changed over time.[46] This approach openly contradicts at least one of the pillars of media development: the effort to create enabling regulatory environments for media systems to grow stronger and more open in developing countries. In China, as in many other states, the law has been regularly used to shape and direct the evolution of domestic media systems. In the case of new media, whose regulation has been shared by different ministries for a long time, the use of the law to both enable and restrict specific uses and applications has even exceeded what has been the case in Europe and in the United States.[47] The Chinese government, however, has refrained from suggesting that regulatory measures adopted in China should be adopted by other countries to inform their own media policies, or even that regulation per se should be the mechanism through which specific outcomes should be achieved.[48]

Per the financial instruments adopted with its development partners, China, which is not a member of the DAC, has distinguished itself from other donors, as it "does not separate ODA from economic cooperation or investment as long as the intent is to expand local capacity."[49] As Deborah Brautigam has pointed out, most of Chinese finance is actually provided in the form of export credits, non-concessional state loans and aid used to foster Chinese investment, none of which fit into the official definition of ODA, but nonetheless have a "developmental" goal, as they support projects identified by recipient countries as instrumental for promoting "economic development and welfare." As she and other scholars have insisted, discarding these instruments – which in OECD parlance would largely be considered OOF – would risk missing important, possibly the most important, implications of China's rise as a development actor.

Following Brautigam's exhortation towards understanding China's aid in its own terms, rather through the lens of external standards,[50] the next sections let the modes of operation that have characterized China's presence in the media and telecommunications sectors in Africa emerge from empirical evidence first, considering a broad range of initiatives involving both public and private Chinese actors. I only secondly ask which aspects bear similarities with the approaches championed by other donors and which others constitute instead a new mode of engagement.

This analysis, in resonance with studies surveying other sectors, indicates that projects that do comply both with mainstream definitions of media development and with aid are relatively marginal. They consist mostly in support to state media, especially state broadcasters. The largest share of resources, instead, has been going towards financing Africa's information infrastructure, in ways that do fit within the broader goal of strengthening access and capacity as per the conception of media development, but are largely supported through OOF. Finally, the venture of China's own media in Africa, as a tool for public diplomacy, does not comply with either definitions (media development or aid), but interestingly rides over some issues that in previous decades characterized the debate on media development, including the strengthening of South–South cooperation and the promotion of a developmental model of journalism.

Aid with state-strings attached

"Aid with no strings attached" has become one of the slogans of China's approach to development, the most evident feature used to assert its distinctiveness from Western conceptions of aid. A survey of Chinese assistance in the ICT sector indicates this approach has been consistent in the policy realm, where Chinese authorities have exercised little or no pressure to promote reforms or shape the regulatory environment.[51] But when it comes to the types of actors China has supported, through grants, training, and provision of equipment, it appears that Chinese support has overwhelmingly flowed towards the state, indicating a consistent selection bias in distributing resources.

While most other donors have espoused an issue-based approach, seeking to sustain specific agendas first and selecting which partners in each country could best help achieving certain goals – be it a local NGO, a private company, or a specific ministry – China has preferred an actor-based approach, seeking to increase the capacity of the state. There could be a rationale behind this strategy. In the end, in countries such as Uganda and Ghana, the establishment of strong and relatively independent state media (as had been the case for the newspapers *The New Vision* and *The Daily Graphic*) has led to greater professionalism and engagement among different factions once the market was liberalized.[52] However, the analysis of the ways in which China has disbursed funds to state media, independently from their professionalism and performance, indicates how this form of support is more the expression of a diplomatic use of aid, as a way to please partners, than of a calculated strategy aimed at rewarding a successful, strategic use of state media by African governments. A few examples may help make this point clearer.

In Zimbabwe, a 2012 deal on economic and technical cooperation with China, worth 1.14 billion yuan (around US$180 million), included loans of 31.5 million yuan (around US$5 million) to provide television broadcasting vans to the Zimbabwe Broadcasting Corporation (ZBC).[53] In February 2013, China donated a broadcasting van in a bilateral governmental meeting in Harare, alongside agreements for food and infrastructural loans.[54] As well as helping to cement bilateral relations between the two states, the vans contributed to the broadcasting capacity of the national ZBC broadcaster, which previously had to hire such equipment privately. This equipment also helped to digitize Zimbabwe's broadcasting network, thus helping to meet the June 2015 continent-wide deadline for digital switchover set by the International Telecommunication Union back in 2006. In Liberia, China spent US$4 million on radio expansion, in cooperation with the Liberia Broadcasting System (LBS), in 2008.[55] An agreement between the Chinese and Liberian governments in 2012 provided the LBS with technical assistance for satellite transmission, broadcasting equipment, and interpretation; the government of China also helped with the cost of renting the transmitting satellite for two years.

Most initiatives aimed at supporting local media comply with both the definitions of media development and aid indicated above. They are focused on building the capacity of state media, albeit selectively, and they are largely provided in the form of grants and donations of equipment and training. As in the case of other sectors, however, Chinese flows that do comply with definitions set by Western donors represent only a very small portion of China's overall contribution.

The shaping of Africa's information infrastructure

The largest share of Chinese resources in the media and telecommunications sector has been channeled towards supporting Africa's information infrastructures. Similar to what had been the case with roads and railways, in many countries in Africa China has emerged as one of the most important actors in also ensuring connectivity in the digital realm. The significance of the contribution to developing terrestrial and mobile information infrastructures, however, has varied widely from country to country, and China has displayed a significant ability to fit in and adapt to preexisting markets and regulatory environments.

Chapter 3 will examine at length the cases of Ethiopia, Kenya, Ghana, and Rwanda, but China's support in developing communication infrastructure and providing value-added services has spanned across the whole continent. In Guinea, Exim Bank loans have supported the state-owned Societé des Telecoms de Guinée (SOTELGUI), expanding its fiber optic infrastructure.[56] In Nigeria, Exim Bank offered Nigeria a US$100 million loan for the development of its Galaxy Backbone ICT network, to boost "the sophistication and effectiveness of the government's efforts to tackle security challenges."[57] In 2010, Exim Bank supported e-government projects in Ghana with two concessionary loans, worth US$30 million and US$150 million.[58] In Tanzania, Chinese concessionary loans funded the construction of the National ICT Broad Infrastructure Project.[59]

Projects funded by China in the telecommunications sector appear compliant with one of the principles of media development, namely the support of infrastructure and capital equipment, even if some specific traits of Chinese approach deserve particular attention. Historically, support to telecommunications has seldom figured in media development projects, in most cases because of the sheer amount of resources needed to make a difference in this area – notable exceptions are the Leland Initiative, which already in 1996 received US$15 million to provide Internet connectivity to some selected African countries,[60] and infrastructural projects supported by the World Bank.[61] China's ability to act as a very large lender, however, has set it apart from most other donors. In addition, media convergence has made understanding the ripple effects that infrastructural investments may have on a plurality of media increasingly difficult. The same content can be accessed through different channels, and most interactive spaces that are transforming communication in Africa are emerging precisely at the crossroads between traditional and new media and telecommunication (as represented, for example, by interactive radio talk shows, where participation is ensured by audiences calling, sending SMS, posting on a show's Facebook page, or writing to its Twitter handle).[62]

On the contrary, when considered through the parameters set by the DAC for ODA, China's assistance in this area cannot be accounted as aid. Loans to support telecommunications are in fact usually provided either in the form of concessionary loans offered by the China Exim Bank or China Development Bank to African governments, but tied to having a Chinese company implementing the project, or of export credits offered directly to Chinese companies, which use them to implement a project envisioned by a national government.

Public diplomacy or development journalism?

Another important area where China has made inroads into Africa is the expansion of its own media, including CCTV, Xinhua, and *China Daily*. Initiatives such as these are usually comprised under the rubric of "public diplomacy," which is separated from media development, and is funded in ways that cannot be accounted for either as ODA or as OOF. Also, in this case, however, China's approach presents challenges to mainstream definitions and categorizations. When CCTV Africa (later rebranded as China Global Television Network – CGTN) launched on January 12, 2012, it became the largest non-African TV initiative in Africa. It employed more than 100 journalists, mostly African, between its headquarters in Nairobi and reporting from across the continent. Building on its considerable resources, CCTV/CGTN Africa was the only international TV initiative to guarantee one hour of original reporting from Africa every day, targeting African and global audiences. One year later, this was increased to one and a half hours, split into two tranches and featured globally on CCTV/CGTN News. CCTV/CGTN Africa added to a long list of previous Chinese media initiatives on the continent. In Kenya, China Radio International (CRI) had launched its own local FM stations in three East African cities, broadcasting in English, Mandarin, and Swahili, also providing A.M. channel coverage across the country.[63] State news agency Xinhua, whose presence in Africa dates back to the 1950s, also significantly expanded its scope and reach in Africa in the 2000s and 2010s, and its news stories have begun to appear regularly in national newspapers.[64] In 2012, the same year CCTV/CGTN Africa started operating, the state-controlled English-language newspaper *China Daily* launched its Africa Weekly edition, the "first English language newspaper published in Africa by a Chinese media enterprise."[65]

These initiatives are aimed at different targets and seek to improve the image of China among African audiences in more or less direct ways. Agencies such as Xinhua tend to be seen as closer to state interest,[66] while international broadcaster CCTV/CGTN Africa has been more innovative.[67] Most of them, however, share some common traits. With relation to the debates highlighted above, the most relevant is the emphasis placed on the idea of "developmental journalism." Chinese media actors have been insisting on a conception that positions the media at the center of a country's efforts to build the state, the nation, and guarantee better development prospects. This position is remarkably in line with UNESCO's past efforts to create a New World Information and Communication Order (NWICO), which represented one of the apexes in the debate on media development, stressing South–South cooperation and the ability of voices coming from the Global South to be heard and affect global narratives. This is also a conception that has found resonance among some of the African journalists working in the Chinese media. As Douglas Okwatch, an experienced Kenyan producer working for CCTV/CGTN Africa, explained:

> A lot of debate has been going on in this country about watchdog journalism. In the 1980s and 1990s during the transition period we required a more aggressive style of journalism, we required watchdog media and we were working to produce change. This change came more slowly than we expected but it eventually came. The media freedom is there now. And now the question is different. Now the question is about the use that we can make of the space that we created. Now it is not the time for fighting as much as before. Now we have to play a better role in promoting growth in our countries, in promoting development.[68]

This conception of a distinctive model of journalism shared by some Chinese and African journalists working for CCTV/CGTN Africa, however, seems to struggle to find a concrete application in everyday reporting. As the few analyses of the content broadcast by CCTV/CGTN Africa – mostly through its news program Africa Live – indicate, the Chinese channel does not dramatically distinguish itself from other international broadcast-ers, in terms of reporting conflicts and crises.[69] CCTV/CGTN may offer a different spin on certain news, and be more critical of Western initiatives and interests, but it still struggles to find a narrative that is at the same time appealing and different from the aggressive styles of journalism championed by channels such as Al Jazeera, which have become increasingly popular among African audiences.[70]

This third area of China's entrance into the media sector in Africa seems therefore to still exist outside of the boundaries of what is defined as media development, but it is a space to watch. There seems to be a commitment on the side of Chinese editors to develop a distinctive narrative, building on ideas of South–South cooperation, leveraging the image of Africa as a continent of opportunities, but Chinese channels abroad seem not to have found – yet? – a distinctive image and space that does appeal to African and global audiences.

Chinese technology and investments beyond state support

Dani Madrid-Morales and Herman Wasserman, analyzing the case of Chinese media engagement in South Africa,[71] have warned about the risks of focusing on Chinese involvement exclusively as media assistance or aid, even when it is analyzed and unpacked using frameworks aimed at understanding the specific nature of China's entrance, rather than applying external categories. Especially in complex and large African markets such as South Africa and Nigeria, a large share of Chinese involvement has been of a commercial nature, including investing in African media companies and producing and distributing content for the local market, rather than the result of government-sponsored programs.

Even enlarging the focus to other – smaller – African mar-kets, it has become increasingly common to find examples of Chinese companies that have either graduated from the need to secure loans from Chinese banks to compete with other, more established brands, or have operated outside of a privileged rela-tionship with the Chinese government from the outset. As the next chapter will discuss with greater detail, in Kenya, Huawei has been contracted by the country's largest mobile operator, Safaricom, to build a fiber optic backbone in competition with the one that was being built by the Kenyan government, in ways that resemble the project signed by South African operator Cell C with ZTE a few years earlier. Handset manufacturers, such as Hong Kong-based Tecno, have tailored their products towards markets where electricity supply may not always be taken for granted and environmental factors may require tougher designs, rapidly acquiring large shares in Kenya, Nigeria, Rwanda, and Tanzania.[72] StarTimes has become a leading actor in guiding transition from analogue to digital television in Africa and offering competitive packages in the satellite TV segment in numerous countries on the continent, including Kenya, Rwanda, and Ghana.

While specific contracts may be of a purely commercial nature, testifying the progress made by China's tech companies developing increasingly innovative solutions at competitive prices, it is still important to consider how in most cases these contracts have been signed with companies whose entrance in African markets have been heavily subsidized by the Chinese government or whose support may still be demanded to serve strategic political goals, when needed. This is the case, for example, of a StarTimes project launched in rural Nigeria in 2017 to provide satellite television in areas with limited infrastructure, and framed by the Chinese government as a result of the commitments made at the sixth FOCAC meeting in South Africa in 2015.[73] In an ever-more complex web of ICT initiatives in Africa, it has become increasingly difficult to distinguish projects as purely commercial or purely the result of aid and foreign policy, and it is important to follow the threads connecting different technologies and actors together, as well as closely examining how they are discursively presented to local and foreign audiences.

Conclusion

The examination of the motifs and means underpinning China's expansion in Africa's ICT sector offers a first glimpse of the country's unique strategy, and how it sets it apart from other donors that have sought to influence the regional and global Internet agenda. While firmly rooted in China's own experience with telecommunications and Internet development, this strategy has been able to evolve over time, adapting to unique national contexts. This evolution has produced different, sometimes conflicting, responses among African partners. Some have praised the Chinese government and Chinese companies for their willingness to support locally rooted versions of the information society, adapting to markets still in evolution. Others have accused China of using Africa as a testing ground to learn lessons that can later turn useful in other contexts, a stepping stone in China's rise as a global Internet superpower.

The following chapter seeks to offer fresh evidence to bring clarity to this debate, digging deeper into cases where China has significantly contributed to the development of the local ICT sector, interacting with different types of political and technological regimes.

Notes

1 The carrier was the most powerful of the family of Long March rockets, purposefully built to launch communication satellites into orbit, but also the one that lifted China's first lunar lander in 2013.

2 Jim Yardley, "Snubbed by U.S., China Finds New Space Partners," *The New York Times*, May 24, 2007, sec. International/Asia Pacific, www.nytimes.com/2007/05/24/world/asia/24satellite.html.

3 Kevin Pollpeter, *Building for the Future: China's Progress in Space Technology during the Tenth 5-Year Plan and the US Response* (Maroon Ebooks, 2015).

4 Yardley, "Snubbed by U.S., China Finds New Space Partners."

5 Todd Moss and Sarah Rose, "China ExIm Bank and Africa: New Lending, New Challenges," *CGD Notes*, 2006, http://mercury.ethz.ch/serviceengine/Files/ISN/38231/ipublicationdocument_singledocument/12344342-ee55-4679-8955-d27614b78bf4/en/2006_11_06.pdf.

6 Stephen, "Chinese Rocket Launches Powerful Nigerian Satellite into Orbit," *Space*, www.space.com/13975-china-rocket-launching-huge-nigeria-satellite.html.

7 "Nigeria's Space Program: A Rare Glimpse Inside the West African Nation's Satellite Operation," *International Business Times*, www.ibtimes.com/nigerias-space-program-rare-glimpse-inside-west-african-nations-satellite-operation-1411236.

8 ITU, *Key ICT Indicators for Developed and Developing Countries and the World*, www.itu.int/en/ITU-D

/Statistics/Documents/
statistics/2018/ITU_Key_2005-
2018_ICT_data_with%20
LDCs_rev27Nov2018.xls.

9 "Who's Afraid of Huawei?" *The Economist*, August 4, 2012, www.
economist.com/node/21559922.

10 Aaron L. Friedberg, *"Going Out": China's Pursuit of Natural Resources and Implications for the PRC's Grand Strategy*, vol. 17, 3 (National Bureau of Asian Research, 2006); Nargiza Salidjanova et al., *Going Out: An Overview of China's Outward Foreign Direct Investment* (US-China Economic and Security Review Commission, 2011).

11 David Wolf, *Making the Connection: The Peaceful Rise of China's Telecommunications Giants* (Wolf Group Asia, 2012).

12 "Who's Afraid of Huawei?"

13 Interview: Myriam Said, Director of Programmes and Service Delivery, Global Computing Solutions (GSC). Addis Ababa, Ethiopia, May 10, 2013.

14 Interview: ICT Expert. Addis Ababa, Ethiopia, May 9, 2013.

15 Interview: Ehizogie Binitie, Co-Founder, Rancard Solutions. Accra, Ghana, August 19, 2010.

16 Interview: Phares Kariuki, Entrepreneur. Nairobi, Kenya, April 29, 2013.

17 Howard W. French, *China's Second Continent: How a Million Migrants Are Building a New Empire in Africa* (Vintage, 2014), 17.

18 Benjamin Tsui, "Do Huawei's Training Programs and Centers Transfer Skills to Africa?" China Africa Research

Initiative (Johns Hopkins, 2016), http://static1.squarespace.com/
static/5652847de4b033f56d2bdc29/
t/578e94e83e00be6595
4feb3f/1468962026573/
Tsui+brief+v.5.pdf.

19 Interview: Cao Wenji, Public Relations, Huawei. Nairobi, Kenya, May 2, 2013.

20 Claire van den Heever, "Huawei's Quest for Hearts and Minds in Africa," *Asia Times*, 2016, www.atimes.com/article/huaweis-
quest-hearts-minds-africa.

21 Kenneth King, *China's Aid and Soft Power in Africa: The Case of Education and Training* (James Currey, 2013); Kurlantzick, *Charm Offensive*; Willy Lam, "Chinese State Media Goes Global: A Great Leap Outward for Chinese Soft Power?" *China Brief* 9, no. 2 (2009): 2–4; Joseph Nye, "Why China Is Weak on Soft Power," *The New York Times*, January 17, 2012, sec. Opinion, www.
nytimes.com/2012/01/18/opinion/
why-china-is-weak-on-soft-
power.html.

22 David L. Shambaugh, *China Goes Global: The Partial Power* (Oxford University Press, 2013), 26.

23 Iginio Gagliardone, "China as a Persuader: CCTV Africa's First Steps in the African Mediasphere," *Ecquid Novi: African Journalism Studies* 34, no. 3 (2013): 25–40; Iginio Gagliardone and Pál Nyíri, "Freer but Not Free Enough? Chinese Journalists Finding Their Feet in Africa," *Journalism* 18, no. 8 (2017): 1049–1063.

24 Interview: Asnake Kefale, College of Social Science, Addis

Ababa University. Addis Ababa, Ethiopia, January 4, 2012.

25 Mogopodi Lekorwe et al., "China's Growing Presence in Africa Wins Largely Positive Popular Reviews," *Afrobarometer*, 2016, http:// afrobarometer.org/publications/ wp117-african-perspectives-china-africa-gauging-popular-perceptions-and-their-economic.

26 Lekorwe et al., "China's Growing Presence in Africa."

27 Interview: Marketing Manager, StarTimes. Nairobi, Kenya, September 11, 2012.

28 Interview: Engineer, Ghana Broadcasting Corporation. Accra, Ghana, August 22, 2010.

29 Yun Sun, "Africa in China's Foreign Policy" (Brookings, 2014), www.wlv.ac.uk/media/departments/ faculty-of-social-sciences/ documents/Africa_in_China_ Brookings_report.pdf.

30 Sun, "Africa in China's Foreign Policy," 19.

31 Forum on China-Africa Cooperation, *Beijing Action Plan (2007–2009)*, www.fmprc.gov.cn/zflt/ eng/zyzl/hywj/t280369.htm.

32 China's Second Africa Policy Paper, www.chinadaily.com.cn/world/ XiattendsParisclimateconference/ 2015-12/05/content_22632874.htm.

33 Amare Asrat, "Ethiopian, Chinese Parties Agree to Strengthen Relationship," *Fana Broadcasting Corporate*, 2017, www.fanabc. com/english/index.php/news/ item/9868-ethiopian,-chinese-parties-agree-to-strengthen-relationship;

Makwaia Wa Kuhenga, "The Alliance between Tanzania's CCM and China's CPC," *China Daily*, 2017, http:// wap.chinadaily.com.cn/2017-03/24/ content_28664166.htm.

34 Wa Kuhenga, "The Alliance between Tanzania's CCM and China's CPC."

35 Iginio Gagliardone, "Media Development with Chinese Characteristics," *Global Media Journal* 4, no. 2 (2014): 1–16.

36 Allen and Stremlau, "Media Policy, Peace and State Reconstruction"; Guy Berger, "Problematizing 'Media Development' as a Bandwagon Gets Rolling," *International Communication Gazette* 72, no. 7 (2010): 547–565; Shanthi Kalathil, "Scaling a Changing Curve: Traditional Media Development and the New Media," *CIMA*, 2008, http://cima.ned.org/ publications/research-reports/ scaling-changing-curve-traditional-media-development-and-new-media#sthash.s3rzgycq.dpuf; Krishna Kumar, "International Assistance to Promote Independent Media in Transition and Post-Conflict Societies," *Democratization* 13, no. 4 (2006): 652–667; Mary Myers, "Donor Support for Media Development," in *Whose Voices? Media and Pluralism in the Context of Democratisation*, ed. L. Rudebeck and M. Melin (University of Uppsala, 2008).

37 Iginio Gagliardone, "From Mapping Information Ecologies to Evaluating Media Interventions: An Experts Survey on Evaluating

Media Interventions in Conflict Countries," Report published by United States Institute of Peace (USIP), Washington, DC, 2010; Myers, "Donor Support for Media Development."

38 Kalathil, "Scaling a Changing Curve"; Kumar, "International Assistance to Promote Independent Media in Transition and Post-Conflict Societies."

39 Berger, "Problematizing 'Media Development' as a Bandwagon Gets Rolling."

40 Kalathil, "Scaling a Changing Curve."

41 Myers, "Donor Support for Media Development."

42 DAC 2003 as quoted in Deborah Brautigam, "Aid 'With Chinese Characteristics': Chinese Foreign Aid and Development Finance Meet the OECD-DAC Aid Regime," *Journal of International Development* 23, no. 5 (2011): 752–764.

43 Brautigam, "Aid 'With Chinese Characteristics.'"

44 Alberto Alesina and David Dollar, "Who Gives Foreign Aid to Whom and Why?" *Journal of Economic Growth* 5, no. 1 (2000): 33–63; Anke Hoeffler and Verity Outram, "Need, Merit, or Self-Interest: What Determines the Allocation of Aid?" *Review of Development Economics* 15, no. 2 (2011): 237–250.

45 Axel Dreher and Andreas Fuchs, "Rogue Aid? The Determinants of China's Aid Allocation," *Courant Research Centre: Poverty,*

Equity and Growth-Discussion Papers, 2011, www.econstor.eu/handle/10419/90522.

46 Stephanie Kleine-Ahlbrandt and Andrew Small, "China's New Dictatorship Diplomacy: Is Beijing Parting with Pariahs?" *Foreign Affairs* 87, no. 1 (2008): 38–56.

47 Rogier Creemers, "The Privilege of Speech and New Media: Conceptualizing China's Communications Law in the Internet Era," 2014, http://papers.ssrn.com/sol3/papers.cfm?abstract_id=2379959.

48 William A. Callahan, *China: The Pessoptimist Nation* (Oxford University Press, 2009); Shambaugh, *China Goes Global.*

49 May Tan-Mullins, Giles Mohan, and Marcus Power, "Redefining 'Aid' in the China–Africa Context," *Development and Change* 41, no. 5 (2010): 862.

50 Brautigam, "Aid 'With Chinese Characteristics.'"

51 Fackson Banda, "China in the African Mediascape: A Critical Injection," *Journal of African Media Studies* 1, no. 3 (2009): 343–361; Xiaoling Zhang, "How Ready Is China for a China-Style World Order? China's State Media Discourse under Construction," *Ecquid Novi: African Journalism Studies* 34, no. 3 (2013): 79–101.

52 Iginio Gagliardone, Nicole Stremlau, and Daniel Nkrumah, "Partner, Prototype or Persuader? China's Renewed Media Engagement with Ghana," *Communication, Politics & Culture* 45, no. 2 (2012), http://

mams.rmit.edu.au/xbo3w37se3t8z.
pdf; Nicole Stremlau, *The Press and
Consolidation of Power in Ethiopia
and Uganda*, PhD thesis, London
School of Economics and Political
Science, 2008, http://etheses.lse.
ac.uk/2160/.

53 Xinhua, "China Extends
Economic Assistance to Zimbabwe,"
Xinhua, April 7, 2012, www.focac.org/
eng/zxxx/ t925720.htm.

54 Xinhua, "Visiting Chinese
Commerce Minister Signs
Agreements with Zimbabwe,"
Xinhua, February 22, 2013,
www.china.org.cn/world/
Off_the_Wire/2013-02/22/
content_28036524.htm.

55 Yu-Shan Wu, *The Rise of
China's State-Led Media Dynasty
in Africa* (South African Institute of
International Affairs, 2012).

56 TeleGeography, "Huawei
Bags Guinean Backbone Contract,
Sotelgui Rescue Plans Ongoing,"
TeleGeography, 2013, www.
telegeography.com/products/
commsupdate/articles/2013/01/03/
huawei-bags-guinean-backbone-
contract-sotelgui-rescue-plans-
ongoing/.

57 Francis Ndubuisi, "FG, China
Exim Bank Seal $600m Deal on
Abuja Light Rail, Galaxy Backbone,"
This Day Live, September 13, 2012,
www.thisdaylive.com/articles/
fg-china-exim-bank-seal-600m-
deal-on-abuja-light-railgalaxy-
backbone/124857.

58 Iginio Gagliardone, Maria
Repnikova, and Nicole Stremlau,

"China in Africa: A New Approach
to Media Development?" (Oxford,
2010), https://global.asc.upenn.edu/
publications/china-in-africa-a-new-
approach-to-media-development/.

59 Pius Rugonzibwa, "Tanzania:
China Aid to Boost National
Budget," *Tanzania Daily News*,
March 27, 2013, http://allafrica.com/
stories/201303270063.html.

60 USAID, "USAID/Leland
Initiative Home Page," November
9, 2001, https://web.archive.org/
web/20011109164754/http://www.
usaid.gov/leland/.

61 Vivien Foster and Cecilia
Briceño-Garmendia, *Africa
Infrastructure Country Diagnostic*
(World Bank, 2009), www.
energytoolbox.org/library/infra2008/
references/34_12-17-08_africas_
infrastructure_foster.pdf.

62 Iginio Gagliardone, "'Can You
Hear Me?' Mobile–Radio Interactions
and Governance in Africa," *New
Media & Society* 18, no. 9 (2016):
2080–2095; Florence Brisset-
Foucault, "Radio, Mobile Phones, Elite
Formation and Sociability: The Case
of Uganda's 'Serial Callers,'" 2013,
https://papers.ssrn.com/sol3/papers.
cfm?abstract_id=2250539.

63 Wu, *The Rise of China's State-
Led Media Dynasty in Africa*.

64 Xin Xin, "Xinhua News
Agency in Africa," *Journal of African
Media Studies* 1, no. 3 (2009):
363–377.

65 China Daily, "China Daily
Launches Africa Weekly Edition,"
China Daily, December 14, 2012,

www.chinadaily.com.cn/china/2012-12/14/content_16016334.htm.

66 Yuezhi Zhao, "The State, the Market, and Media Control in China," in *Who Owns the Media*, ed. Zaharom Nain and Pradip Thomas (Zed Books, 2004), 179–212.

67 Gagliardone, "China as a Persuader."

68 Interview: Douglas Okwatch, Producer of Talk Africa, CCTV/CGTN Africa. Nairobi, Kenya, September 12, 2012.

69 Vivien Marsh, "Chinese State Television's 'Going Out' Strategy: A True Global News Contraflow? A Comparison of News on CCTV's Africa Live and BBC World News TV's Focus on Africa" (China's Soft Power in Africa: Emerging Media and Cultural Relations between China and Africa, Nottingham University's Ningbo campus, 2014); Zhang, "How Ready Is China for a China-Style World Order?"

70 Geoffrey York, "Why China Is Making a Big Play to Control Africa's Media," *The Globe and Mail*, September 11, 2013, www.theglobeandmail.com/news/world/media-agenda-china-buys-newsrooms-influence-in-africa/article14269323/; Zhang, "How Ready Is China for a China-Style World Order?"

71 Madrid-Morales and Wasserman, "Chinese Media Engagement in South Africa."

72 Justina Crabtree, "'China Is Everywhere' in Africa's Rising Technology Industry," *CNBC*, July 28, 2017, www.cnbc.com/2017/07/28/china-is-everywhere-in-africas-rising-technology-industry.html.

73 Olatunji Saliu and Zhang Baoping, "China Initiates Satellite TV Project in Rural Africa," 2017, http://news.xinhuanet.com/english/2017-08/11/c_136517844.htm.

3 | INNOVATIVE DEMOCRATS AND DEVELOPMENTAL STATES

The Chinese do not really have a China–Ghana or China–Zambia policy. They deal with the continent as a whole, even if they are starting to understand the diversity within the continent. So for China the general strategy is there, they know the areas where they are ready to invest. Then it is up to the individual country to choose their specific area of cooperation.[1]

A continental overview of China's engagement in the ICT sector, as offered in the previous chapter, corroborates the impression that China is not trying to impose a blueprint in shaping information societies in Africa. Rather, as suggested above by Ghana's former Ambassador to China, Beijing's willingness to expand its sphere of action to new communication technologies has produced specific and individual responses in different African countries, each seeking to make use of Chinese financial and technical support to bolster relatively unique development projects.

The absence of a one-size-fits-all strategy for ICTs in Africa, however, does not rule out the possibility that patterns are emerging in the way in which China's aid, loans, and export credits are producing results in different types of African countries. Is China engaging differently in democratic and authoritarian states? To which extent do the relative strength of the state, private companies, or civil society organizations influence the outcomes of projects developed in collaboration with the Chinese government or with Chinese companies?

By analyzing the cases of two democracies, Kenya and Ghana, and two autocracies, Ethiopia and Rwanda, with whom China has developed increasingly strong ties, this chapter begins to offer elements to answer these questions, also stressing the importance of not singling China out, but considering a broader set of changes that have recently come to shape the development of ICTs in Africa.

Resilient and distinct political projects

Within contemporary Africa, the development trajectories charted by Kenya, Ghana, Ethiopia, and Rwanda have attracted significant regional and global attention. Sustained economic growth – averaging 5.9% in Kenya, 7% in Ghana, 7.6% in Rwanda, and 10.6% in Ethiopia in the period between 2005 and 2015[2] – has granted each of them a position among Africa's Lions, the term coined by financial institutions to identify Africa's most promising economies, in the footsteps of Asia's Tigers.[3]

Kenya has become a poster child of the information revolution in Africa, hosting some of the most popular initiatives combining new communication technologies and local demands, including the mobile money service M-PESA and crowdsourcing tool Ushahidi. Ghana has attracted praise for its democratic credentials, signaled by the ability of elections to ensure regular and relatively smooth transitions of power between the two leading political parties. Ethiopia and Rwanda have more controversially emerged as examples of aspiring developmental states, combining the commitment of the political and economic elite towards sustained growth with an authoritarian grip on power.

When considered in pairs, through the lenses of their political institutions, Kenya and Ghana on one side, and Ethiopia and Rwanda on the other, display significant similarities. Polity IV has consistently ranked Rwanda and Ethiopia as closed anocracies, countries occupying an intermediate position between democracies and autocracies, while Ghana and Kenya have been included among the world's democracies. The Bertelsmann Transformation Index has similarly placed the two pairs in two distinctive categories, even if with a more pessimistic outlook: Ethiopia and Rwanda have been considered hardline autocracies, and Ghana and Kenya defective democracies. Other rankings, such as *The Economist*'s Democracy Index and Freedom House's

Freedom in the World, while applying the same labels to Ethiopia and Rwanda (categorized as authoritarian and not free, respectively), have tended to place Ghana slightly above Kenya. Ghana has been flagged as a flawed democracy by *The Economist* and free by Freedom House, while Kenya has been labeled as a hybrid regime and part-free. All nations have showed limited variation in the past few years.

While the four countries have displayed comparable patterns of growth and, when considered in pairs, remarkably similar political institutions, when analyzed through the lenses of the – less definite – categories that have been used to chart the relationship between China and Africa, they present significant variations that can be used to better understand China's interests and behaviors in the continent. Among the four, Ghana is the only country with significant natural resources. Already an oil producer in the 1960s and 1970s, the discovery of a massive offshore oilfield in 2007 projected Ghana into a new league of large oil exporters, with China trying to secure a privileged position in the exploitation of new reserves. Ethiopia and Rwanda, with their limited resources and small consumer base, have been referred to in recent literature on China–Africa relations as unusual cases for China's interest.[4] But they are also countries where the similarity of the political projects and some resilient aspects of ideological bonds between China and Africa – along the path of a socialist political project – seem to have played a bigger role. Kenya, apparently the country with the least to offer to China in terms of resources and similarities in the political sphere, is the country where the Chinese government has decided to install all its major media operations, including the headquarters of CCTV/CGTN Africa, Xinhua, and *China Daily*.

By examining China's behavior in the ICT sectors in Kenya, Ghana, Ethiopia, and Rwanda, the next sections seek to bring to light similarities and differences that have characterized the approach followed by the Chinese government and Chinese companies in each of these countries, and to examine the relationships China has developed with different types of actors involved in the shaping of national information societies.

Africa's innovative democrats – Kenya and Ghana

Already in the 1990s, when the Internet begun to emerge as global phenomenon, and the first mobile phones hit the consumer market, Ghana and Kenya arose among the most active innovators in their respective regions, a role they have continued to hold ever since.

Ghana was the first country in sub-Saharan Africa to develop a cellular mobile network. Under the brand name Mobiltel, Millicom International Cellular begun to offer the service already in 1992. Ghana was also a pioneer in privatizing telecommunications, opening the market in 1996 as part of a broader process of reform and restructuring of state-owned companies.

When compared to Ghana, Kenya – destined to become probably the most talked about country in Africa when it comes to digital innovation – initially adopted a more timid approach towards ICTs. The Kenya Communication Act put an end to the monopoly of the state-run Kenya Posts and Telecommunication Corporation (KPTC) only in 1998. The transition that ensued was marred by chaos and delays, with multiple companies seeking to secure a spot as competitors of the national operator, but seeing their bid canceled as a result of mismanagement and conflicts between different public institutions.[5]

This slower start, however, was followed by a rapid evolution, turning Kenya into possibly the most influential regional player in Africa in the ICT sector. Kenya took a leading role in projects that dramatically improved Internet availability and affordability in East Africa, through the docking of four fiber optic submarine cables to its coast in 2009, 2010, and 2011, and the progressive creation of a wide terrestrial infrastructure connecting Kenya to its neighbors. Also, in the ICT policy sector, Kenya acted as a prime mover, launching the East Africa Internet Governance Forum in 2008, the first IGF to be established at a regional level.

Over time, both countries have become possibly the most visible embodiments in Africa of the multi-stakeholderism celebrated in international fora as the most effective approach to connect a plurality of actors to create vibrant and inclusive information societies.[6] International organizations, private companies, national and international civil society groups, and the state played different but complementary roles in leading subsequent phases in the evolution of ICTs.

Multiple stakeholders, cooperation, and conflict

Especially in the early stages of the diffusion of the Internet and mobile telephony, the leaders of Ghana and Kenya displayed a marked inclination to adopt policies and exhortations coming from *regional and international organizations*. In both countries, the World Bank played a pivotal role in encouraging the first waves of liberalization and in shaping ICT policies aimed at opening the market up, leading to the privatization of state-owned companies and the creation of a relatively competitive telecommunication market. Following the lead of the African Information Society Initiative, launched at the United Nations Economic Commission for Africa (UNECA), Ghana was among the first countries in Africa to develop a National Information and Communication Infrastructure (NICI) strategy, seeking to develop an action plan for creating an inclusive information society.

Liberalization allowed a plurality of national, regional, and international *private operators* to begin competing for increasingly profitable markets, driving down prices and allowing experimentation in value-added services. As Levi Obonyo, as Director of the Media Council of Kenya, explained, answering a question about the ideology that drove the development of the Internet in Kenya:

> The debate is very much driven by business. A lot of the measures that are being debated are about lowering the costs, innovating services. Kenya did not go along with what was happening in the region and took its own way. It opened up, it liberalized. Other countries, even South Africa, tried to protect the national telco, and as a result they are still lagging behind. Kenya did not and this was a great advantage.[7]

Ghana acted even faster than Kenya in opening up the market and allowing competition. As a result, both countries soon became battlefields for national and international operators to acquire shares and customers, including investors from India (Bharti Airtel), Kuwait (Zain), South Africa (MTN), and the UK (Vodafone). Most international telecom companies quickly adapted to the features characterizing Ghana and Kenya's consumer base, converging towards prepaid – rather than contract-based – schemes for voice, messaging, and eventually data. Some companies went a step further, seeking to exploit untapped opportunities offered by local markets. This was the case of M-PESA, Africa's most successful mobile money service. Launched in 2007 by Safaricom, tapping into funding made available by the UK's Department for International Development (DFID) for joint investments to improve access to financial services, it quickly became Kenyans' preferred system for transferring money across the nation, and one of the most common ways to pay for ordinary transactions.[8]

The year 2007 was also when Kenya's most contested, and violent, elections took place. The uncertainty emerging from the ballots led to protests, violent mobs, and killings.[9] These events shook the country and led radio and television to temporarily interrupt reporting, fearing that news about ongoing violence could fuel retaliations across the country. They also motivated a group of Kenyan computer scientists and entrepreneurs to develop a new system for people with access to a computer or mobile phone to log incidents, so that they could be plotted on a map and allow following the evolution of the situation in real time. Known as Ushahidi ("Testimony" in Swahili), the system was later deployed thousands of times to map crises on a global scale, from earthquakes in Haiti and Japan, to electoral contests in Nigeria, to wildfires in Italy, further contributing to the image of Kenya as a global hub for innovation.[10]

The people behind Uhsahidi were part of a larger network of Kenyan activists who embraced digital media as a way to bring reform, in society and in politics. *Civil society* has represented in fact another fundamental pillar that has contributed to the definition of the uses and application of new technology in Kenya. Over time, Kenya has carved itself a space in Africa for the vibrancy of its online debates, mixing humor, demands for transparency, and the ability to act on scandals and crises. The hashtag #KOT (Kenyans on Twitter) has become a rallying point for Kenyan citizens to come together and denounce cases of corruption and mismanagement, or promote new campaigns. The Kenyan civil society has also become a driving force regionally, leading the institution of the East Africa Internet Governance Forum, and becoming a guide for other members of the civil society and public sector in the region to introduce digital innovation in their respective countries.[11]

Finally, but not less importantly, the *Kenyan state*, while initially trying to protect national champions and vested interests (e.g. Telecom Kenya), has progressively become a proactive driver and facilitator of digital innovation. Key individuals, such as Permanent Secretary Bitange Ndemo, were able to strike a delicate balance between convincing public institutions to open up and involving a plurality of actors in the development of Kenya's information society. The long excerpt below summarizes the trajectory followed by the Kenyan state in charting a relatively distinctive conception of information society:

> Up until 2005, the Internet was seen as a tool for subversion. In public offices fax and computers were not allowed and seen as counterproductive. But then we started developing a plan to make ICTs part of our development. First we wanted to be like India. We started with this idea of competing for jobs and investing in outsourcing. India was the outsourcing capital of the world. But then we went a different way.
>
> We decided to invest in content and applications. And we had a hit because of M-PESA. Initially the central bank did not want to let M-PESA operate. I then said I would take personal responsibility. But there were a lot of other people saying that we needed new projects and to invest in data.
>
> So we progressively moved from the idea of outsourcing to internal efficiency and improving our governance model. That was my uphill task. My selling points were: we have the infrastructure; we have kids doing amazing things, coming up with new applications. I am now pushing to create applications

so that every person can have access to data. And we can also create value out of data.[12]

While less talked about regionally and internationally, Ghana has followed similar steps in the creation of a relatively inclusive national information society, connecting and balancing the influence of different stakeholders. While Kenya had Ushahidi as its most globally well-known application, Ghanaian activists and entrepreneurs made the headlines for their efforts to develop applications able to spot fake medicines that had been flooding West African markets.[13] Similar to Kenya for East Africa, Ghana also played a leading role in establishing the West Africa Internet Governance Forum as a regional node seeking to promote multi-stakeholder partnerships in the region.[14]

The relative openness that came to characterize the evolution of ICTs in both countries, however, also came at a cost. In some cases, these costs were related to the destabilizing forces unleashed by new forms of communication, allowing a plurality of actors to assert competing agendas, also through exploiting existing tensions within society. In others, they depended on the contradictions inherent in the very multi-stakeholder model promoted internationally and variously embraced at the national level.

Open societies, and their fractures

Multi-stakeholderism has had numerous supporters, and some powerful critics, with the Chinese government possibly emerging as the most vocal and influential. As the next chapter will illustrate, China's ambition has been to present multilateralism, with its more formal articulation of relations between states and intergovernmental institutions, as a better route towards governing the Internet. When considering the appeal of different models of Internet regulation among actors that are likely to be norm-takers rather than norm-makers, as is the case of the four countries considered here, it is also important to stress how some of the key challenges to multi-stakeholderism have not come just from influential critics, but also from within.

One of the most powerful, and empirically grounded, illustrations of the fragilities of multi-stakeholderism, especially as promoted in the Global South, comes from Jenna Burrell's account of the participation – or lack thereof – of the Ghanaian civil society in the regional conference promoted by the World Summit on the Information Society (WSIS) in Accra in 2005.[15] The event, as others organized as part of the WSIS process, was preceded by bold claims about the inclusiveness of the proceedings and the importance of ensuring broad participation.

As Burrell has illustrated, however, rather than actively seeking out and engaging with potentially critical but knowledgeable members of Ghana's emerging information ecosystem – such as coalitions of owners of for-profit Internet cafés, which in 2005 still constituted the most common venue for Ghanaians to access the Internet – the organizers behaved like "ventriloquists," involving organizations that were indeed local, but whose voice and jargon closely resembled the organizers themselves. As she has explained, drawing on her ethnographic work in Accra, "I have no record of the term information society ever being uttered by any of the Internet café owners, operators, and users I encountered in the course of fieldwork."[16] Being unable to speak the appropriate language, "the Internet cafés and their users remained invisible to the regime of development."[17] Instead, "the particular language used by the so-called civil society groups present at the WSIS reaffirmed an institutional discourse rather than challenging it on any fundamental level."[18]

My own experience as organizer, participant, and observer of events of the kind held in Accra makes Burrell's account very familiar.[19] The hypocrisy highlighted by the WSIS event is a constitutive, rather than marginal, component of the broader process of norm-making that has characterized not only attempts to shape a global information society, but numerous other issue areas. Neither is limited to the tokenism displayed in the participation allowed for the local civil society, but extends to more powerful actors, including governments in developing countries. As Henry Farrell and Martha Finnemore have poignantly argued, reflecting on the role of hypocrisy in American foreign policy, and in multilateral institutions more broadly:

This system needs the lubricating oil of hypocrisy to keep its gears turning. To ensure that the world order continues to be seen as legitimate, U.S. officials must regularly promote and claim featly to its core liberal principles, [but] Washington is unable to consistently abide by the values that it trumpets.[20]

Farrell and Finnemore have pointed at the leaks by Manning and Snowden as threats to this system,[21] for their dramatic display of the double standards that underpin it. China, as more fully argued later in the book, represents an additional threat, especially for its ability to call bluff. The recollection of a Ghanaian technocrat of how his government sought funds to build a national fiber optic infrastructure offers a concrete illustration of China's ability to exploit these contradictions:

> The idea was to support a backbone company owned by the government. We approached the EU and USAID, but there was a problem with the financing because they wanted the company owning the backbone to be private, while for us it had to be government-owned. They did not understand that in Africa the government is the prime actor in development. Our idea was that a telecommunication infrastructure is like a highway.
>
> The EU and USAID would not come in if it was not private. But for us the problem was that the private would not provide the social services. But the Chinese were ok. They accepted to support Ghana's broadband infrastructure facility to promote our information society.
>
> If you look at the WSIS declaration of principles, the commitment is to produce and create assets, distribute and consume to improve the living conditions of humankind. So those components were there. And the only way developing countries can participate in the information society is to build infrastructure. But the US is not committed to build infrastructure. But in Ghana we wanted an expensive state-of-the-art backbone all over the country.[22]

Here, and during the rest of the interview, it was interesting to notice how this civil servant, who had participated in the WSIS process and seemed committed to the principles that emerged from it, felt betrayed by how these principles were not respected by some of the very actors that led the process. China, on the other hand, seemed more inclined to respond to Ghana's demands, quietly, but in a way that displayed nonetheless the inability of other donors to abide to their own standards.

Openness, destabilization, and violence

The other critical element that emerged from the acceptance and implementation of a relatively open conception of the information society was the unleashing of forces able to take advantage of the opportunities offered by ICTs to serve divisive, and potentially destructive, agendas. The case of Kenya's 2007 elections has already been introduced. Vernacular radios were more instrumental than digital media in fueling animosity between different ethnic groups,[23] and yet unprecedented levels of hate and dangerous speech were registered in most social networking platforms.[24] The violence in Kenya also became an opportunity for other regimes, which had adopted a more closed and restrictive approach towards ICTs, in partial defiance of international pressures, to defend and justify their decisions. As an international civil servant explained, referring to negotiations with the Ethiopian government about the liberalization of telecommunications:

> We discussed a lot with the Ethiopian government but they said, "Not now" [...] Now they can use Kenya as a justification. And say, "You see? We told you that this technology can be used for violence in Africa. There are people ready to use technology to destabilize." So they are afraid, it is a strategy, they want to move slowly, to be given time for implementing technology in a way that is not dangerous for them.[25]

Despite eventually resulting in a peaceful transition of power, the elections in Ghana in 2008 were also preceded by fears that the media could fuel violence between supporters of opposing parties and different ethnic groups. As a Ghanaian political commentator and supporter of the New Patriotic Party (NPP) explained:

There is a danger about the uses made of the freedom we have in Ghana. I think that we got close to civil war in 2008 because of the media. There were live broadcasts accusing people in government of staffing ballot boxes in their houses. There was no ethics. So when I read that Ghana is a success story I think, "Wait a moment." In the end the civil war did not happen because the opposition won. But it was close.[26]

The destabilizing potential of unrestrained media is another area China could have exploited to advance its own approach towards increasing access while maintaining control. However, Chinese authorities and companies have tended to keep a relatively low profile, aiding governments when asked, but without visibly asserting a contrasting model to deal with the Internet's disruptiveness.

Is China helping African democracies to expand their information space?

Coming relatively late into the evolution of the Internet in Ghana and Kenya, China had to relate – in principle – with existing networks of technologies, actors, and discourses, and with attempts to assert specific, and often conflicting, conceptions of the information society. However, rather than becoming embroiled in these debates and negotiations, seeking ways to promote its own version of what the role of ICTs should be, or to publicize its generous contribution, the Chinese government – and the Chinese companies operating in the two countries – adopted a relatively subdued approach, getting straight into implementing what the Kenyan and Ghanaian governments had requested.

The strategy followed by China was remarkably similar in the two countries, emerging at the intersection of its own predilection towards supporting infrastructural projects and the ambition of the Kenyan and Ghanaian governments to build stronger foundations for their information societies. In both cases, China's Exim Bank was instrumental in making funds available to an extent that was beyond the reach of most other donor countries, and Chinese companies were contracted to carry out the projects.

In Ghana, in addition to the support sought to expand infrastructure, the government also made use of available funds to develop one of the most ambitious e-government projects in West Africa. At a cost of US$180 million, provided by Exim Bank through two concessionary loans of US$30 million in 2008 and US$150 million in 2010, the project was aimed at first reaching the coastal cities and then centers in the north of the country, ensuring public administrations, schools, and hospitals would be the first to benefit from enhanced connectivity. Huawei was awarded the technical realization of the project while Ghana's National Information Technology Agency (NITA) was tasked with overseeing the project's implementation, which combined different solutions to adapt to the varying conditions characterizing Ghana's topography. While connections among the main cities as well as the network in the capital consisted largely of fiber optics, other metropolitan areas were connected through a WiMAX technology, and remote areas relied on satellites and other leased terrestrial circuits. The six Regional Coordinating Councils were equipped with teleconferencing facilities that, according to NITA, were "all connected to the presidency to provide communication links with the presidency promoting effective and efficient governance."[27] A national data center, built in the president's office, was placed at the center of the system to coordinate all communications and provide secure data storage facilities.

The collaboration between China and Kenya followed a similar trajectory, even if in this case it was Chinese companies that made the first steps, bidding and winning contracts to expand connectivity across the country. Huawei and ZTE, together with the French company Sagem, contributed to creating Kenya's first National Optic Fibre Backbone Infrastructure (NOFBI), bringing high-speed connectivity to the main urban centers and allowing a first series of e-government projects to be delivered regionally.[28] The country was split into three sections, Western Kenya, Coast and North Eastern, and Nairobi and Central – each region handled by one company. Sagem laid out cables in Coast and North Eastern, Huawei in Nairobi and Central, and ZTE in Western Kenya. A second round of NOFBI (known as NOFBI II) was directly funded with Chinese resources. In 2012, China's Exim Bank provided a US$71 million loan to support further extension to 36 administrative district centers across the country, with the objective of also allowing people in remote areas to access faster Internet. A condition for the loan was that the implementing agency had to be Huawei.[29]

The commonalities and differences of China's approach in Kenya and Ghana are analyzed later in this chapter, after having also introduced the cases of Ethiopia and Rwanda, but one observation is particularly relevant here. Rather than adopting a template approach, the Chinese government and Chinese companies displayed a remarkable ability to adapt to the conditions encountered in each country. As indicated earlier, both Ghana and Kenya have been characterized by an open market, where a plurality of actors competed and gained influence in different sectors. This quality was also displayed in how the projects characterized by a significant Chinese involvement were configured.

In the case of Ghana, while both phases of the e-government network infrastructure were funded by Chinese loans and Huawei was the implementing partner, it was ultimately Vodafone that became the owner and manager of the infrastructure.[30] In addition, in subsequent phases, other donors were allowed to join in and contribute to the effort of expanding information infrastructure. In 2015, the Danish government offered a US$38 million concessionary loan to implement the Eastern Corridor Fiber Optic Backbone Infrastructure Project, further extending connectivity in more remote parts of the country.[31] In Kenya, the fiber optic network installed by Huawei and ZTE was administered in such way that could be shared by different actors, public and private, to offer services but also guarantee revenues. As Bitange Ndemo, Permanent Secretary for Information and Communication, explained:

> NOFBI was built as an open access platform. If it had just been for the government it would have been expensive. We decided that the infrastructure had to be shared. Because everybody is doing their own thing. One company is digging here, the other is digging

there. So they started to understand that it may be more effective to share the cables and work all together. But you still needed the state, because there are areas such as Northern Kenya that are not covered because there is little population so there is not the incentive. We wanted to have an open platform with a partnership between private and public. This is what I mean with open. But not everybody appreciated the concept. We had to create a consensus among the different partners. Many people do not understand that the government has to facilitate the private sector.[32]

In Kenya, Chinese companies were not contracted exclusively as part of state-sponsored projects, but managed to also be competitive in the private sector. Soon after the signing of the agreement for NOFBI II, Kenya's leading telecom operator, Safaricom, decided to invest US$95 million to build an additional 2,400 km fiber optic cable to support its growing customer base. A large share of the contract was assigned on a commercial basis to Huawei, which had already worked in collaboration with Safaricom to roll out the 4G network. A remaining share of Safaricom's expansion project was assigned to Ericsson.[33]

Africa's authoritarians and their ambitions towards a "developmental" Internet

Compared to Kenya and Ghana, Chinese involvement in the ICT sector in Ethiopia and Rwanda could not be more different, for two – opposite – reasons. In Ethiopia, China has become the single largest supporter of the relatively unique vision of the national information society elaborated by the Ethiopian People's Revolutionary Democratic Front (EPRDF), the country's leading coalition. Without Exim Bank's concessionary loans, exceeding US$3 billion, Ethiopia would have probably never been able to realize what no other country in Africa had achieved before, significantly expanding Internet and mobile access in a regime of state monopoly. In Rwanda, on the contrary, China played almost no part in supporting ICTs, while significantly increasing its presence in other key sectors, from manufacturing to terrestrial infrastructure.[34] It was South Korea, instead, that became instrumental in supporting the Rwandan government's plan to dramatically increase access to new communication technologies, following a pattern, however, that closely resembles the one charted by China in other countries in Africa.

The difference in how China supported ICT development in Ethiopia and Rwanda becomes even more puzzling when faced with the striking similarities shared by the two countries, including how they are fitting into China's broader strategic expansion on the continent. Ethiopia and Rwanda are often paired in debates about development and democratization in Africa. They both emerged from violent civil wars led by ideologically driven guerrilla groups; they have developed a love–hate relationship with donor countries, receiving substantial amounts of aid while advocating distinctive ideas of development that partially challenge mainstream policies; and their ruling elites have succeeded at staying in power through multiple electoral contests, maintaining a relatively high level of legitimacy. As Frederick Golooba-Mutebi and I sought to explain elsewhere,[35] and I further elaborate below, the Ethiopian and Rwandan governments have also shared similar conceptions of the role ICTs should play in national development, placing the state at the center of innovation, and considering it a primary beneficiary of the efficiency gains new technology can produce.

From the top to the bottom

Ethiopia and Rwanda have been increasingly portrayed as significant contemporary examples of African states ruled by elites who have been able to combine centralized authority, long-horizon planning and neo-patrimonial and clientelist practices in ways that facilitate long-term investment and the use of rents for growth-generating activities.[36] The power accumulated by the state has been invested in projects that could buy legitimacy and a longer time horizon for the ruling elite to implement its political ambitions. Over time, Internet-based projects (e.g. e-government platforms enhancing the accountability of local leaders) have begun to play an increasingly important role in this scheme.[37]

As has been the case in other developmental states in Asia,[38] the decision to invest in ICTs as a symbol of progress and a source of legitimacy within a context where political competition is limited came from the very top. As the late Prime Minister of Ethiopia Meles Zenawi remarked:

> Not long ago, many of us felt that we were too poor to afford to invest seriously in ICT. We assumed that ICT was a luxury that only the rich could afford [...] We did not believe that serious investment in ICT had anything to do with facing the challenges of poverty that kills. Now I think we know better. Now we believe we are too poor not to save everything we can and invest as much of it as possible on ICT. We recognize that while ICT may be a luxury for the rich, for us – the poor countries – it is a vital and essential tool for fighting poverty.[39]

Similarly, Rwanda's President Paul Kagame asserted that:

> In Africa, we have missed both the agricultural and industrial revolutions and in Rwanda we are determined to take full advantage of the digital revolution. This revolution is summed up by the fact that it no longer is of utmost importance where you are but rather what you can do.[40]

As John Rwangombwa, the Governor of the National Bank of Rwanda and former Minister of Finance, further explained:

> With Vision 2020 we wanted to turn Rwanda into a service led economy supported by innovation. ICT is a key enabler for that also for other sectors. As a landlocked country our future is in the service industry. The president was the one who had the big role in pushing this agenda. He himself has a passion for IT. With this kind of leadership the other players fell into line.[41]

The Minister of Education and founder of the Kigali Institute of Technology (KIST), the institution that trained the first IT graduates in post-genocide Rwanda, added how the roots of President Kagame's interest for new technology had to be found in the guerrilla struggle:

The president understood in the old days how technology helped in the struggle to coordinate people. And now he is interested in using technology for peaceful purposes. [...] But also his travels in places like Singapore, Korea, Hong Kong. The answers he got there were important. These countries were investing not only in ICTs but also in teaching mathematics. And we took inspiration from that.[42]

The commitment shown towards making use of the Internet, and ICTs in general, to support the developmental project has, however, taken significantly different forms in Ethiopia and Rwanda. In Rwanda, technocrats have been given more room to decide how to realize the visions articulated by the top leadership and, at least at relatively high levels of the state apparatus, they have been entrusted the power to implement projects without continuously seeking political approval. In Ethiopia, instead, politics has largely prevailed over technical expertise. ICTs have been embraced as a tool that could ensure policies developed by the top leadership could be streamlined down to the lowest levels of the administration, but minimizing room for interpretation and localization.

The state above all

The strategy elaborated by the EPRDF-led government to shape the Internet in Ethiopia has been fairly distinctive in Africa. While most countries on the continent slowly overcame their skepticism towards liberalizing Internet provision, only to later introduce regulatory or technical mechanisms to contain the tensions these measures unleashed, the Ethiopian government decided from the very beginning to sacrifice access for control and security. In the 1990s, when the first initiatives to promote Internet access in Africa began to take shape, in Ethiopia, as elsewhere on the continent, there were great expectations regarding the Internet's potential. Eventually, however, it was the government's concerns that prevailed in defining the initial and future steps that the Internet would take in the country.

The initiative launched to structure Ethiopia's first moves in the Internet era, aptly called BITE – Bringing Internet to Ethiopia – is a vivid example of this approach. Initiated in 1995 by Dawit Yohannes, the Speaker of the House of Peoples' Representatives, BITE was aimed at producing concrete recommendations on how policymakers could handle the Internet effectively. Similar to what had happened in Ghana and Kenya, initial debate took cues from multi-stakeholderism, benefiting from the active participation of representatives from NGOs and professional bodies, who were trying to strike a balance between the hype coming from the West and the initial skepticism and conservatism shown by the EPRDF. As Dawit Bekele, one of the most active advocates for an open and inclusive use of ICTs, described his own involvement in BITE:

> At the time nobody knew about the Internet. From Ethiopia we did not even have access to the Internet, so we could not have access to relevant information for the BITE commission. But we made a series of recommendations anyways. [...] We had realized that the government would have not accepted a privately owned Internet provider, so we proposed to have a flexible system under ETC.[43]

The system Dawit refers to was a public network service provider, a "not-for-profit service organisation with the main objective of serving the public and developing services,"[44] independent from any actor in particular and accessible to all. The concept was not far from what would have later informed the large infrastructural projects China supported in Kenya and Ghana. The Ethiopian government, however, rejected the idea and decided to place service provision under its direct control.

This was only the first of a series of frustrations the private sector and the civil society faced in their attempts to import tools, regulatory norms, and best practices emerging at the international level. The efforts made by actors other than the government to develop a more dynamic information environment were strongly opposed. This reaction was motivated by the need to slow down the pace of transformation in order to exert more control over it and by the desire to occupy the new political space that was created by the Internet in ways that would primarily benefit the government and its national project.

The state in Rwanda played a similarly critical role in shaping the evolution of the national information society, but it did so in ways that more closely resemble the path followed by other developmental states, forging cooperative relationships with the private sector, rather than seeking ways to centralize and direct every aspect of the development of ICTs.[45] In an initial phase, given the absence of strong and skilled private firms at the local level, this meant finding ways to lure in foreign companies that, alongside the pursuit of a profit, would also buy into key aspects of the developmental project articulated by the government of Rwanda.

The first example of this strategy was the investment that Tri-Star, a company affiliated to the Rwandan Patriotic Front (RPF), Rwanda's ruling party, made to facilitate South Africa's mobile operator MTN's entrance into the country's telecommunication market, as a sole provider of mobile connectivity – until 2006.[46] Attracting MTN to Rwanda was no easy task. The company was approached after efforts to attract other international telecoms such as Vodacom and Telcel, a smaller regional player based in the Democratic Republic of Congo, had failed. The majority of the initial capital MTN used came from Rwandan sources, via Tri-Star. MTN therefore came in as a minority investor, bringing in mainly new technology, while the Rwandans bore the bulk of the risk of investing. MTN reckoned that with the country's small market, it would take years before it would turn a profit. The prediction was proved wrong only two years after it set up shop, with early success propelling it to venture into neighboring Uganda as well.

The approach followed in the case of Tri-Star/MTN became almost paradigmatic in guiding the involvement of the government of Rwanda in the ICT sector. Rather than taking direct responsibility for the development of ICTs in the country, or forging too close relationships with just a few private actors, the government chose to step in and intervene every time it realized a specific partnership or project was not leading decisively enough towards the goals it had set. This was the case of the creation of Broadband Systems Corporation (BSC), a nominally private

Internet service provider in which the government of Rwanda is a majority shareholder. As one of its founders explained:

> The government wanted more. MTN laid down the fiber to the border. But the government really wanted decentralization and each district to have fiber. So, we were given the mandate to connect every district, also those that did not make financial sense. [...] At the beginning it was not done with a commercial idea. The government wanted to serve itself and its own needs.[47]

BSC was mandated to offer high-speed connectivity to the public administration, in order to allow e-government projects to be streamlined across the country, but also to drive prices for broadband down, buying bandwidth from international suppliers at wholesale rates. A few years after the establishment of BSC, and once the company had seemingly fulfilled its mandate, the government of Rwanda moved on to forge yet another new partnership, this time with Korea Telecom, to equip the country with next-generation mobile connectivity.

The strategy to attract different partners to support the government's vision of the information society has not been limited, however, to international corporations and skilled entrepreneurs. As Laura Mann and Elie Nzayisenga have vividly illustrated,[48] adapting Simone's concept of "people as infrastructure" to explain the rapid diffusion of mobile telephony across the country,[49] in order to ensure the uptake of mobile connectivity, the government allowed telecoms to rely on a diffused network of airtime resellers, in contravention to its otherwise strict policy on street hawkers. The airtime sellers interviewed for the research were confident about the contribution they offered in the expansion of the mobile network, and displayed a remarkably positive attitude towards their future. As Mann and Nzayisenga noted, however, the sellers also seemed unaware of the diminishing role they were likely to play in the near future, as the result of the government's broader plan for the expansion of ICTs. As they explained, "while unregulated sellers helped telecommunication companies to achieve their rapid rates of penetration at the dawn of mobile telecommunications, they may be not be so suitable for the next stage of its development."[50]

The strategy elaborated by the government of Rwanda thus proved successful in finding allies to embark on different phases in the evolution of ICTs, but also led to progressively abandoning partners that had lost momentum in contributing to the latest stages in the evolution of the national information society. During interviews at companies such as BSC, it was palpable how its employees felt the government had moved on, investing in a new, higher-profile partnership with Korea Telecom to build a new-generation network, while providing little certainty about their own future.

New development allies: China and South Korea

As already discussed for the cases of Ghana and Kenya, one of the most dramatic contradictions of the international ICT agenda, as promoted by international organizations and Western donors, has been to portray ICTs as a powerful response to many development challenges, but then fail to follow up on these very proclamations and adequately support developing countries realizing their own ambitions in the ICT sector. As a Rwandan cadre in charge of managing donor relations for the Minister of Finance explained:

> When we decided to invest in the backbone, the argument
> the donors were putting forward against this decision was:
> Why fibre when you do not have electricity? They did not take
> our ambitions to become an ICT hub seriously. They said,
> "Forget it," and all sort of arguments were put forward. Their
> counterproposal was giving us some money to improve
> the VSAT.[51]

China and South Korea, countries that had themselves dramatically benefited from the opportunities opened by the information revolution, responded differently to these types of ambitions, cementing a stronger sense of solidarity among partners in the Global South.

On November 8, 2006, Chinese telecom giant ZTE and the Ethiopian Telecommunication Corporation signed the largest agreement in the history of telecommunications in Africa. Backed by China Development Bank, ZTE offered a loan of US$1.5 billion (to which it added US$0.4 billion for engineering) to overhaul and expand Ethiopia's telecommunications system. The loan, to be repaid over 13 years, was disbursed in three phases. The first phase had a particularly symbolic value. Branded the "Millennium Plan," it was expected to produce its results – laying down more than 2,000 km of fiber optic cable connecting Ethiopia's 13 largest cities – by September 11, 2007, the day marking the beginning of the new millennium on the Ethiopian calendar.[52] The second and third phases similarly focused on infrastructure development, expanding coverage to rural areas, and building the capacity of the system to support 20 million mobile users (from the initial 1.2 million) and more than a million Internet broadband users.[53] Resources also went towards upgrading the Ethiopian government's ambitious e-government and e-learning projects, WoredaNet and Schoolnet, allowing some public administrations and schools served by the two systems to progressively switch from expensive and inefficient satellite connections to terrestrial broadband.

China's support has allowed the Ethiopian government to reach goals no other African country had achieved before, dramatically expanding access in a regime of monopoly. Elsewhere in Africa, the liberalization of the market was what drove expansion in coverage and lowering costs. Countries that opted for a system tightly controlled by the state, such as neighboring Eritrea, have severely lagged behind in developing information infrastructure and services. By providing capital, equipment, and the expertise, all with no strings attached in terms of policy changes (e.g. liberalizing the market), ZTE not only brought the Ethiopian government out of the cul-de-sac in which it had put itself by stubbornly defending monopoly; it also helped it realize its vision of a tightly controlled but developmentally oriented national information society.

On June 7, 2011, the now rebranded Ethio Telecom issued a tender to further boost the capacity of Ethiopia's mobile phone network to 50 million subscribers by 2015 and to introduce 4G connectivity in selected areas. The tender was similarly based on a vendor-financing scheme, as had previously been the case with ZTE. However, in contrast to 2006, the tender was public and various companies competed. As the *Wall Street Journal* put it, however, "again, financing won the day, with the two [ZTE and Huawei] pledging a total of US$1.6 billion. Western equipment suppliers, such as Ericsson and Alcatel Lucent SA, couldn't match the Chinese offer."[54] With the signing of two separate contracts of US$800 million each with Huawei and ZTE, competition was introduced in the shape of a rivalry between two Chinese companies that have been contending for shares of the Chinese market for a long time. As a representative of Huawei in Ethiopia, who requested to speak on condition of anonymity, argued:

> It is normal that Huawei and ZTE compete for resources. ZTE in Ethiopia did not do a good job. It did not have enough incentives. So the government asked Huawei to come, because we have a better reputation in Africa.[55]

China's contribution therefore served not only to support the unique vision elaborated by the EPRDF, but also to introduce and experiment with limited forms of competition that would not threaten the government's hegemonic position in shaping Ethiopia's information society.

As mentioned earlier, the strategy adopted by the government of Rwanda facilitated the emergence of a relatively less centralized network of actors and technologies, but led to comparable outcomes. Korea Telecom had initially come into Rwanda simply as a contractor to lay down part of the national fiber backbone project, starting with the 130 km Kigali Metropolitan Network (KMN). In 2013, however, the relationship between Korea Telecom and the government of Rwanda was stepped up, taking the form of a joint venture under the name of Olleh Rwanda Networks (ORN). ORN's goals were twofold: rolling out 4G connectivity reaching 95 per cent of the population by the end of 2018, and providing IP-based services to public and private institutions. Under the terms of the contract, Korea Telecom was expected to invest US$140 million a year in the project for an accumulated investment of approximately US$2.1 billion over 25 years.[56] The government, on its part, gave access to its 3,000 km national fiber optic networks, providing 175 MHz of spectrum, and granted Korea Telecom an exclusive license for 25 years.[57]

As Pansik Shin Ngenzi, ORN's CEO, explained, the joint venture was an indication of how Korea Telecom and the government of Rwanda shared a similar vision and were ready to take some risks to see it realized. In his own words:

> Rwanda took the right approach. The quicker the better. It is true, you have problems like electricity. You have to get the right balance between short-term needs and long-term vision. Something can be a luxury now, but in the long run we need skills. The ICT development is important to transform this country from agricultural based to service based. It is also good for this society to brand itself as a smart society. In this market they are looking forward to the 4G. There are big expectations. If I can use a single word I would say this is the "right shortcut" to reach Vision 2020. But we have also to admit that we have not seen the returns yet.[58]

Rwanda represented an opportunity for a country such as South Korea – relatively small but at the forefront of innovation in the digital domain – to test new possibilities in Africa. As ORN's CEO continued, "We want to expand to other countries. Other countries in Africa are looking at Rwanda as an example. And the fact that we have localized a solution in Rwanda can help us then tailor for another African country."

For South Korea as a whole, investing in Africa represented an opportunity to display its increased international role, experimenting in an area – digital innovation – that was relatively familiar. Partially as a result of the public–private partnership between Korea Telecom and the government of Rwandan, the South Korean embassy, which was closed in the aftermath of the Rwandan genocide, reopened in Kigali. As a Korean diplomat in Kigali explained:

South Korea does not have a strong presence here in Africa. But right now in South Korea many more people recognize the importance of Africa. We have opened a new emphasis. Rwanda for us is a very good target country also to show to our own people in Korea that both private investment and aid can have good results.[59]

South Korea's size and national budget would make it impossible for the country to compete with China in Africa. And yet the financial exposure of Korea Telecom in Rwanda (US$2.1 billion over 25 years) is not far from what China committed to support the Ethiopian government's ambitions in the ICT sector. Even more interesting, some central components of the projects realized by ORN bear striking similarities with what Chinese companies realized not only in Ethiopia, but also in Kenya and Ghana. As ORN's CEO explained:

From the beginning, when Korea Telecom first came here, the priority was to connect government offices, schools, hospitals, plus a more affordable fare for the fiber. There is a need for IT supported solutions, like e-government solutions. We want to offer both the system and the skill transfer. This is a condition for the government. The PPP [public–private partnership] is twofold. We have a strong partner but we do not want just to import and localize. The government wants to be a big customer to ensure that the infrastructure serves its needs. In the past different departments were dealing with different companies from different countries, but we are bringing coordination so they will mostly have to deal with us.[60]

Similar to the case of Ethiopia, in Rwanda external support also meant strengthening the government's ability to oversee the development of ICTs and make direct use of infrastructural resources, serving different functions of the administration, from providing better services to the population, to increasing the opportunities for the center and the peripheries of the state to communicate with one another. In striking resemblance with Ethiopia's WoredaNet, the government of Rwanda invested significant resources and expertise to realize a complex videoconferencing system connecting various nodes of the state administration.[61] The system, relying on fiber optic, allowed ministries in Kigali both to collect information from local administrations and to inform them on key policies and decisions.[62] Thanks to a lucky coincidence, during the videoconferencing session I attended at the Ministry of Local Government in Kigali in 2014, a Rwandan official who had just returned from South Korea explained to public administrators across the country how the South Korean practice of Saemaul resonated with Rwanda's Umuganda and could bear lessons for coalescing energies of local communities to achieve common goals.[63]

Conclusion

The experiences of Kenya, Ghana, Ethiopia, and Rwanda pose a difficult test to those claiming China is promoting a more authoritarian model of the Internet in Africa and globally. Rather, they seem to reaffirm China's pledge to support nationally rooted visions of the information society, whether it is the need expressed by the governments of Ghana and Kenya to strengthen infrastructure as well as the capacity of the state to deliver services in a competitive environment, or the ambition of the Ethiopian leadership to expand access under a regime of monopoly. In all cases, the relationship between African and Chinese actors seems to have been driven by the former rather than the latter, with the Chinese government and Chinese companies offering financial and technical backing to projects envisioned at the local level. The Rwandan case seems to offer particularly strong support to this argument. As explained later in the book, the apparatus of control and surveillance created by the Rwandan government, both proactively and reactively, online and offline, possibly presents the closest similarities with the complex model developed within China to concurrently contain dissent and destabilization and promote allegiance to a specific development model. And yet Rwanda is the only country where China has not built a strong presence – to date – in the ICT sector. China therefore does not seem to have selected specific allies in Africa to reinforce a particular idea of the information society, or to have applied a template approach across the continent. Rather, its engagement in the ICT sector appears to be the result of China's ambition to expand its influence and multiply its allies on the continent.

There is, however, an important element that is found in all countries surveyed, and seems to delineate the contours of a Chinese blueprint, or rather Asian blueprint if South Korea is also considered, towards promoting ICT development in Africa: support has invariably been directed towards the state, rather than other actors involved in the shaping of functioning information societies. As illustrated in the case of Kenya, there have been instances when Chinese companies have been contracted on purely commercial bases, but in these cases contracts have been won because of the companies' competitive edge, and no support – in terms of preferential credit or other incentives – appears to have been provided by the Chinese government.[64] This element problematizes the argument that China is backing locally rooted visions of the information society, and raises important questions on whose agency China is actually helping.

The multi-stakeholderism described earlier in this chapter is not just a normative framework, suggesting an ideal mode of cooperation between state actors, private companies, and the civil society. It also has a descriptive quality, referring to how, in the shaping of functioning information societies, different actors have played different roles at different times, in ways that have been crucial to create an inclusive type of innovation that is not skewed towards the narrow interests of only one set of actors. In the case of Kenya, the private sector played a paramount role in pushing the boundaries of innovation, breaking previous frameworks set by the state to regulate telecommunications and banking. It was the civil society, however, that shifted innovation not just in the direction of better access and greater profits, but also towards the creation of applications and strategies that could keep corruption in check, map ongoing violence, or combat hate speech.

Taking this argument beyond Africa, there is no doubt Internet giants such as Facebook, Google, or Amazon have creatively and disruptively innovated myriad sectors of social, political, and economic life. It was the intervention of a powerful supernational institution, such as the European Union, however, that brought to light how these companies have exploited their global nature to avoid taxation, failing to return to European citizens a due share of the profits made in their countries.[65] Examples of conflicts between different types of actors leading to constructively shaping information societies are countless, from the mobilization of the civil society to stop US legislation that could give extreme powers to the music and movie industry to block online content,[66] to German regulation forcing Facebook to take a more aggressive stance against fake news.[67]

By reinforcing the ability of the state, rather than other actors, to shape the evolution of ICTs, China has been supporting in practice a vision of the role of the media in society that is skewed towards the role played by public institutions. While the interest in building functioning and capable states is not exclusive to China, and has been shared by many other donor countries, this tendency can have potentially harmful consequences when it comes to ICTs. A too powerful state may prevent checks and balances of the kind briefly illustrated above to emerge and function at critical junctures, including around elections, or when new legislation is being proposed. A Chinese government displaying friendliness to whichever government is in place is also emboldening narratives framing China as a friend of Africa, and Western donors as seeking to impose their hegemonic visions on less powerful states. While this dichotomy is the result of a selective reading of the national and international politics of development, bundling together legitimate requests to abide to international standards and paternalistic attitudes towards development blueprints, it has already been gaining ground in countries such as Ethiopia, as exemplified by the case of the imprisonment of bloggers accused to be using social media to incite unrest in collaboration with "foreign human right activist organizations."[68]

To conclude, while the accusation of supporting an authoritarian version of the information society in Africa does not seem tenable in a strict sense, the fact that states are being helped in asserting their own visions and projects over other types of actors may lead to indirectly support this claim in the longer term. China's growing backing certainly puts pressure on African polities to ensure elected leadership is indeed democratic. Or, looking at it from a different angle, its "no strings attached" policy may reinforce incentives towards "capturing" the state, when past experience shows China is willing to support incumbent governments, independently from their democratic records. The following two chapters, examining different conceptualizations of the Chinese Internet, and the growing securitization of development embraced by Western donors, offer further elements to understand whether this form of support may threaten over time the possibilities for open information societies to thrive, or may have other consequences that have not been adequately considered up to now.

Notes

1 Interview: Afare Donkor, Ghana's former Ambassador to China. Accra, Ghana, August 20, 2010.

2 World Bank, "Fact Sheet: Infrastructure in Sub-Saharan Africa," *World Bank*, 2010. http://go.worldbank.org/SWDECPM5S0.

3 It must be noted that while the term Asian Tigers has been consistently used to refer to Hong Kong, Singapore, Taiwan, and South Korea, the definition of Africa's Lions has been much more vague and has been variably attributed to a different set of Africa's nations. Bhorat and Tarp's recent book *Africa's Lions: Growth Traps and Opportunities for Six African Economies* includes Ethiopia, Ghana, Kenya, Mozambique, Nigeria, and South Africa, but not Rwanda. The McKinsey Global Institute, which has been responsible for first popularizing the term, in its most recent report – *Lions on the Move II* – has included only Ethiopia, Rwanda, and Kenya, but not Ghana, among the stable growers.

4 Deborah Brautigam, "Ethiopia's Partnership with China," *The Guardian*, December 30, 2011, www.theguardian.com/global-development/poverty-matters/2011/dec/30/china-ethiopia-business-opportunities; Seifudein Adem, "China in Ethiopia: Diplomacy and Economics of Sino-Optimism," *African Studies Review* 55, no. 1 (April 2012): 143–160, https://doi.org/10.1353/arw.2012.0008; Lily Kuo, "Why Is China Investing So Heavily in a Small Landlocked African Country with Few Natural Resources?" *Quartz*, 2017, https://qz.com/827935/rwanda-is-a-landlocked-country-with-few-natural-resources-so-why-is-china-investing-so-heavily-in-it/.

5 Henry Lancaster, "Kenya: Telecoms, Mobile, and Broadband" (Budde, 2015).

6 Claudia Padovani and Elena Pavan, "Diversity Reconsidered in a Global Multi-Stakeholder Environment: Insights from the Online World," in *The Power of Ideas: Internet Governance in a Global Multistakeholder Environment, Berlin: Germany Land of Ideas*, ed. Wolfgang Kleinwachter, (Marketing for Deutschland, 2007), 99–109; Arne Hintz, "Deconstructing Multi-Stakeholderism: The Discourses and Realities of Global Governance at the World Summit on the Information Society (WSIS)," in *SGIR Pan-European International Relations Conference*, 2007, www.eisa-net.org/be-bruga/eisa/files/events/turin/hintz-sgir_ahintz_deconstructing.pdf; Marc Raboy and Claudia Padovani, "Mapping Global Media Policy: Concepts, Frameworks, Methods," *Communication, Culture & Critique* 3, no. 2 (2010): 150–169.

7 Interview: Levi Obonyo, Director, Media Council of Kenya. Nairobi, Kenya, September 12, 2012.

8 Nick Hughes and Susie Lonie, "M-PESA: Mobile Money for the 'Unbanked' Turning Cellphones into 24-Hour Tellers in Kenya," *Innovations* 2, no. 1–2 (2007): 63–81; Olga Morawczynski, "Exploring the Usage and Impact of 'Transformational' Mobile Financial Services: The Case of M-PESA in Kenya," *Journal of Eastern African Studies* 3, no. 3 (2009): 509–525.

9 Keith Somerville, "Violence, Hate Speech and Inflammatory Broadcasting in Kenya: The Problems of Definition and Identification," *Ecquid Novi: African Journalism Studies* 32, no. 1 (2011): 82–101.

10 For a full list of deployment of Ushahidi, see www.ushahidi.com/about.

11 Brandie M. Nonnecke, "The Transformative Effects of Multistakeholderism in Internet Governance: A Case Study of the East Africa Internet Governance Forum," *Telecommunications Policy* 40, no. 4 (2016): 343–352.

12 Interview: Bitange Ndemo, Permanent Secretary for Information and Communication. Nairobi, Kenya, September 14, 2012.

13 "The African Startup Using Phones to Spot Counterfeit Drugs," *Bloomberg*, July 31, 2015, www.bloomberg.com/news/features/2015-07-31/the-african-startup-using-phones-to-spot-counterfeit-drugs.

14 The first communiqué of the Furum, convened in Accra in 2009, can be accessed at www.waigf.org/publications/article/waigf-communique-2009.

15 Another powerful critique of the contradictions in the ICT for development agenda as promoted by the WSIS has been advanced by Michael Gurstein. As he wrote, "while there has been a very considerable degree of 'talking about' ICTs for Development there has been remarkably little 'talking with' those

who are actually doing the job on the ground." See Michael Gurstein, "Networking the Networked/Closing the Loop: Some Notes on WSIS II," 2005, www.worldsummit2003.de/en/web/847.htm.

16 Jenna Burrell, *Invisible Users: Youth in the Internet Cafés of Urban Ghana* (MIT Press, 2012), 145.

17 Burrell, *Invisible Users*, 154.

18 Burrell, *Invisible Users*, 153.

19 In 2003, I participated in the first phase of the World Summit on the Information Society in Geneva. Between 2005 and 2006, I worked for UNESCO in Addis Ababa, participating in and contributing to organize workshops and conferences in collaboration with the United Nations Economic Commission for Africa on ICTs and education (2005), ICTs and capacity-building (2006), and ICTs and development (2006).

20 Henry Farrell and Martha Finnemore, "The End of Hypocrisy: American Foreign Policy in the Age of Leaks," *Foreign Affairs* 92, no. 6 (2013): 24.

21 Chelsea Manning (born Bradley Manning) released hundreds of thousands of classified documents to WikiLeaks in 2010, revealing numerous abuses of the US Army, including during its operations in Iraq and Afghanistan. Edward Snowden leaked classified information in 2013, offering evidence of the US pervasive global surveillance apparatus. For more, see, for example, Greenwald, *No Place to Hide*.

22 Interview: Issah Yahaya, Director of Policy Planning in the Ministry of Communication. Accra, Ghana, August 19, 2010.

23 Somerville, "Violence, Hate Speech and Inflammatory Broadcasting in Kenya."

24 iHub Research, "Umati Final Report" (Nairobi, Kenya, 2013), www.research.ihub.co.ke/uploads/2013/june/1372415606__936.pdf.

25 Interview: International Civil Servant, United Nations Economic Commission for Africa (UNECA). Addis Ababa, March 13, 2008.

26 Interview: Gabby Otchere-Darko, former Editor of *The Statesman* and Director of the Danquah Institute. Accra, Ghana, August 21, 2010.

27 Haruna Idrissu, Minister of Communication, as quoted in Gagliardone, Stremlau, and Nkrumah, "Partner, Prototype or Persuader?" For more information about the configuration of the system, see http://nita.gov.gh/eGovernment-Network-Infrastructure.

28 See, for example, Mark Okuttah, "Telkom Kenya Set to Run Fibre Network on Behalf of Government," *Business Daily*, June 1, 2010, www.businessdailyafrica.com/Corporate-News/Telkom-Kenya-set-to-run-fibre-network-on-behalf-of-government/-/539550/929626/-/m96mry/-/index.html.

29 See, for example, Margaret Wahito, "Kenya: China to Fund Kenya's Fibre Optic Project," June 28, 2012, http://allafrica.com/

stories/201206290024.html.http://
allafrica.com/stories/2012062
90024.html.

30 Francis Sackitey, "Huawei
Nudges Ghana to E-Government," *This
Is Africa*, 2013, www.thisisafricaonline.
com/Development/Huawei-nudges-
Ghana-to-e-government.

31 NITA, "President Inaugurates
a $38 Million Fiber Optic Backbone
Project," *NITA*, 2015, http://nita.gov.
gh/article/president-inaugurates-38-
million-fiber-optic-backbone-project.

32 Interview: Bitange Ndemo,
Permanent Secretary for Information
and Communication. Nairobi, Kenya,
September 14, 2012.

33 See, for example, Okuttah
Mark, "Safaricom Loosens China's
Grip on Local Contracts with Sh14bn
Tender," *Business Daily*, December 6,
2012, www.businessdailyafrica.com/
Corporate-News/Safaricom-loosens-
China-grip-on-local-contracts/-
/539550/1638364/-/11xotu6z/-/index.
html.

34 Kuo, "Why Is China Investing
So Heavily in a Small Landlocked
African Country with Few Natural
Resources?"

35 Iginio Gagliardone and
Frederick Golooba-Mutebi, "The
Evolution of the Internet in
Ethiopia and Rwanda: Towards a
'Developmental' Model?" *Stability:
International Journal of Security
and Development* 5, no. 1 (2016),
www.stabilityjournal.org/
articles/10.5334/sta.344/.

36 David Booth and Frederick
Golooba-Mutebi, "Developmental

Patrimonialism? The Case of
Rwanda," *African Affairs* 111, no.
444 (July 1, 2012): 379–403, https://
doi.org/10.1093/afraf/ads026; Sarah
Vaughan and Mesfin Gebremichael,
"Rethinking Business and Politics in
Ethiopia," *Africa Power and Politics,
UK Aid, Irish Aid*, 2011.

37 A notable example in both
countries is the use of ICTs to provide
justice at a distance, using satellite
technology and plasma TV screens
to allow judges in the capitals or
in major towns to adjudicate cases
in more remote areas. For more,
see Zenebe Beyene, Abdissa Zerai,
and Iginio Gagliardone, "Satellites,
Plasmas and Law: The Role of
TeleCourt in Changing Conceptions
of Justice and Authority in Ethiopia,"
*Stability: International Journal of
Security and Development* 4, no.
1 (2015), www.stabilityjournal.org/
articles/10.5334/sta.fn/.

38 Chrisanthi Avgerou, *Information
Systems and Global Diversity* (Oxford
University Press, 2002).

39 The Minister of Capacity
Building Tefera Walwa used
this quote from Meles Zenawi
at e-Learning Africa, the first
international conference on ICT for
development, education, and
training in Africa, which took
place in Addis Ababa on May
25–27, 2006.

40 Government of Rwanda, "An
Integrated ICT-Led Socio-Economic
Development Plan for Rwanda,"
GESCI, 2010, www.gesci.org/old/files/
docman/NICIfinal2.pdf.

41 Interview: John Rwangombwa, Governor, National Bank of Rwanda. Kigali, October 22, 2014.

42 Interview: Silas Lwakabamba, Minister of Education. Kigali, October 21, 2014.

43 Interview: Dawit Bekele, Professor at Addis Ababa University and Africa Focal Point for the Internet Society ISOC. Addis Ababa, March 3, 2008.

44 Jane Furzey, "A Critical Examination of the Social, Economic, Technical and Policy Issues, with Respect to the Expansion or Initiation of Information and Communications Infrastructure in Ethiopia," Empowering Socio-Economic Development in Africa Utilizing Information Technology, 1995.

45 Peter Evans, *Embedded Autonomy: States and Industrial Transformation* (Princeton University Press, 1995); Laura Mann and Elie Nzayisenga, "Sellers on the Street: The Human Infrastructure of the Mobile Phone Network in Kigali, Rwanda," *Critical African Studies* 7, no. 1 (2015): 26–46.

46 Mann and Nzayisenga, "Sellers on the Street"; Tim Kelsall, *Business, Politics and the State in Africa: Challenging the Orthodoxies on Growth and Transformation* (Zed Books, 2013); Booth and Golooba-Mutebi, "Developmental Patrimonialism?"

47 Interview: BSC. October 22, 2014.

48 Mann and Nzayisenga, "Sellers on the Street."

49 AbdouMaliq Simone, "People as Infrastructure: Intersecting Fragments in Johannesburg," *Public Culture* 16, no. 3 (2004): 407–429.

50 Mann and Nzayisenga, "Sellers on the Street," 2.

51 Interview: Donor Liaison Officer, Ministry of Finance. Kigali, Rwanda, October 22, 2014.

52 Because of its Coptic tradition, the Ethiopian calendar follows the Julian calendar rather than the Gregorian calendar, which is what is followed by most countries in the world. This means there is a gap of seven to eight years between the two.

53 Gagliardone, *The Politics of Technology in Africa.*

54 Matthew Dalton, "Telecom Deal by China's ZTE, Huawei in Ethiopia Faces Criticism," *Wall Street Journal,* January 7, 2014, sec. World, http://online.wsj.com/news/articles/ SB10001424052702303653004579212 092223818288.

55 Interview: Huawei.

56 Henry Lancaster, "Rwanda: Telecoms, Mobile, and Broadband" (Budde, 2015).

57 Lancaster, "Rwanda: Telecoms, Mobile, and Broadband."

58 Interview: Pansik Shin Ngenzi, CEO, Olleh Rwanda Networks. Kigali, Rwanda, October 24, 2014.

59 Interview: Embassy of South Korea. Kigali, Rwanda, October 23, 2014.

60 Interview: Pansik Shin Ngenzi, CEO, Olleh Rwanda Networks. Kigali, Rwanda, October 24, 2014.

61 I probed in numerous interviewees, from the Governor of the Bank of Rwanda and former Minister of Finance to the Minister of Education, and cadres in the Ministry of Local Government, to understand whether Rwanda's videoconferencing system, which was first launched in 2012, was copied or took cues from Ethiopia's WoredaNet. This hypothesis was supported by the close relationship between the two countries and personal friendship between their leaders. Other projects, such as Ethiopia's Commodity Exchange, did inspire similar ventures in Rwanda. See Igihe, "Ethiopia, Rwanda Discuss Commodity Exchange," 2011, http://business/ethiopia-rwanda-discuss-commodity-exchange. html. The interviewers, however, did not recollect visits to or from Ethiopia to explain the workings of WoredaNet; neither could I find other evidence supporting the case that Ethiopia's system could have influenced the realization of a similar one in Rwanda. Interestingly, however, a very similar videoconferencing project was also developed in Ghana as part of the project sponsored by the Chinese government.

62 Frank Kanyesigye, "Local Govt Leaders Upbeat after Inaugural Video Conference," *The New Times Rwanda*, 2013, www.newtimes.co.rw/section/read/70087/.

63 Saemaul was a practice launched in the 1970s to modernize the rural economy, while Umuganda can be translated as "coming together in common purpose to achieve an outcome."

64 An argument can been made that because of the Chinese government's continuous support towards the expansion of companies such as ZTE and Huawei abroad, as has been the case in Ethiopia, these companies are shouldered in ways that can allow them to better compete abroad in those instances where no direct support is provided by the Chinese government. This can be framed, however, as a mechanism that is more closely related to the relationship between the Chinese government and Chinese ICT companies, rather than as part of its active support of specific African countries.

65 James Kanter, "E.U., Citing Amazon and Apple, Tells Nations to Collect Tax," *The New York Times*, October 4, 2017, sec. Business Day, www.nytimes.com/2017/10/04/business/eu-tax-amazon-apple.html.

66 "SOPA and PIPA Bills Lose Support on Capitol Hill as Google, Wikipedia and Others Stage Protests," *Washington Post*, January 18, 2012, sec. Business, www.washingtonpost.com/business/economy/sopa-and-pipa-bills-lose-support-on-

capitol-hill-as-google-wikipedia-
and-others-stage-protests/
2012/01/18/glQAwIs38P_story.html.

67 Stefan Nicola and Birgit
Jennen, "Germany Gets Really
Serious About Fake News on
Facebook," *Bloomberg*, April
5, 2017, www.bloomberg.com/
news/articles/2017-04-05/

merkel-cabinet-backs-facebook-fines-
to-stem-fake-news-in-germany.

68 Aaron Maasho, "Ethiopia
Charges Nine Bloggers, Journalists
with Inciting Violence," *Reuters*,
April 28, 2014, www.reuters.com/
article/2014/04/28/us-ethiopia-
politics-idUSBREA3R0YC
20140428.

4 | CHINA AS A MODEL?

The multiple faces of the Chinese Internet

China has the most informed people in the world. [Ethiopia] needs the China model to inform the Ethiopian people. – Sebhat Nega, founder of the Tigrayan People Liberation Front[1]

The fact that China is not visibly trying to portray itself as a model to be followed or impose a template to its partners does not prevent others from trying to emulate its policies and achievements. The quote above is from a WikiLeaks cable reporting a meeting between Sebhat Nega, one of the founders of Ethiopia's ruling party and an influential ideologue of the Ethiopian government, and the American ambassador Donald Yamamoto. When I met Sebhat a few years later and asked him about his appreciation for how the Chinese government had been shaping China's communication system, he stressed again – and even reinforced – the remark he previously made with Yamamoto:

> The most informed society in the world is the Chinese. But we cannot reach that level. Nobody can. Everybody in the administration [in China] knows who is who and what needs to be done. And the Chinese leaders are responsive to the demands of the people.[2]

Arguments such as these are still rare, at least in the public domain. China has been publicly praised for its support to Africa's development, but, with a few exceptions,[3] it has not been openly hailed as a model to shape Africa's information societies. As explained later in this chapter, opinions such as those expressed by Sebhat Nega indicate nonetheless how some influential politicians have begun looking more closely at how China has been developing a complex media system, able to contain the destabilizing forces of ICTs while channeling their developmental potential.

But when the drive to emulate the strategies adopted by the Chinese government to shape China's national information society comes from Africa, what elements of China's complex system are considered the most salient? Apart from a few individuals who seemed to have taken a particular interest in China's alternative ideas of the Internet, among the African politicians, entrepreneurs, scholars, and activists I interviewed, there seemed to be little clarity about what a Chinese model of the Internet may actually look like. In the same guise of concepts such as "Beijing consensus," which has been widely debated and used, but has ultimately led to a shallow framing of China's promotion of capitalism without democracy, the prevalent image of the Chinese information society appeared to be one of growth without freedom.

One explanation for this confusion can be found in the chaotic and conflicting nature of the narratives that have emerged around the Chinese Internet. As the first part of this chapter illustrates, competing discourses have been advanced by actors outside of China and by the Chinese government itself, while scholarly efforts to offer a more nuanced understanding of China's information society have largely remained confined to academic debates. Another reason for the confusion around China's information society and its potential relevance for Africa resides in the apparent lack of interest of Chinese actors to explain themselves to African audiences when it comes to media and the Internet. To be sure, as discussed in the second part of this chapter, Chinese authorities have sought ways to push at least one specific discourse – the one supporting the idea of a sovereign Internet – on the international stage. These efforts, however, have been largely confined to specialist forums and diplomatic venues. Little or no attempts have been made to use Chinese media abroad to spin a specific narrative on the Chinese Internet. News concerning the Internet on CCTV/CGTN, Xinhua, or *China Daily* have tended to adopt a generic hyped tone characterizing most tech reporting, featuring the latest innovations and possible advantages for users, without directly engaging with principles and values informing China's information society.

China's *censored* Internet

Technologies such as the Great Firewall, which blocks access to foreign websites and filters cross-border Internet traffic, as well as incidents of the kind leading Google to shut down its Chinese search engine in 2010, have promoted global awareness of the Chinese Internet as a *censored* Internet. Recent developments, including the crackdown on virtual private networks (VPNs), which enabled the most skilled users and many expats to circumvent some of the restrictions placed on content, have further reinforced the image of an all-powerful state seeking to minimize avenues for dissent and contestation.[4]

In 2017, Reporters Without Borders (RSF) described President Xi Jinping as "the planet's leading censor and press freedom predator,"[5] after having included the Chinese government among the "enemies of the Internet" for four consecutive years.[6] Since the launch of the "Freedom of the Net" index in 2011, Freedom House has ranked China among the three worst countries in the world in terms of Internet Freedom, together with Iran and Syria, and as the absolute worst between 2015 and 2017.

Indexes of this kind, while helpful in understanding national and global trends and widely employed in policy and academic circles, have tended to irk not only Chinese authorities, but also Chinese scholars, lamenting the bias of Western organizations applying templates that are unable to capture the complexities of Chinese political and media systems. As Chinese scholar Wang Shaoguang argued:

> The analytical framework of authoritarianism from the West is completely unable to capture deep changes in Chinese politics. In the past several decades, this label has been casually put on China from the late Qing era to the early years of the Republic, the era of warlords, Jiang Jieshi, Mao Zedong, Deng Xiaoping and Jiang Zemin. Chinese politics has made world-shaking changes during this period, but the label put on it made no change at all.[7]

Examining these trends from Africa offers a slightly different picture. African citizens appear to have developed a comparatively more positive perception of China's domestic policies. According to the Pew Research Center, 71% of Nigerians interviewed in 2017 were convinced the Chinese government respects the personal freedoms of its people, and five other African countries featured among those in which the majority of citizens had a positive outlook towards how Chinese authorities handle their citizens' freedoms.[8]

When it comes to the perceptions of Chinese media, and media policies more specifically, large-scale surveys and opinion polls are in short supply, but among the African politicians, entrepreneurs, scholars, and activists I interviewed, the relatively positive perceptions of China's politics and policies at large appeared tamed by the bad name China has acquired because of censorship, surveillance, and the persecution of online activists. As the rector of Ghana's Institute of Journalism, for example, remarked:

> I don't think that the use of the media in the East is very successful. You cannot control too much. The solution is education, you should educate people to use a medium in a certain way. Control is not sustainable in the long term.[9]

For those who had directly entered into partnership with the Chinese government or with Chinese companies to develop ICT projects, as was the case for most government representatives interviewed in Ethiopia, Ghana, and Kenya, there was a certain urgency to explain that China was just one of many partners, and the relation was based purely on economic grounds, without political implications or a desire to follow China's lead in shaping their national information society. In the words of Ghana's Deputy Minister of Information, for example:

> The Chinese are supporting us in digital migration. But we have also received other support, from Sony for example. In general the relationship with China has increased, but it is mostly commercial. There is an honest desire on the side of many African countries to lift themselves from poverty. From the West the funding options are limited and there are also a lot of conditions. But in the case of China it is different. China is

more willing to engage. They have fewer conditions. And our
engagement has been motivated mostly by economic conditions.
This has been the case with all parties in Ghana. If you look
at different governments, they all made deals with China. The
ideological factor has been diluted.[10]

When directly asked whether specific lessons could be drawn from
China, the tendency to stress economics over politics was even
more pronounced. It was particularly so in closed regimes. These
responses resonate with others collected by scholars who have studied China's presence and perception in Africa. As Elsje Fourie, for
example, pointed out in her comparison of Ethiopia and Kenya, it
was as if the leaders of Ethiopia, because of the frequent accusations
of authoritarianism, had to visibly assert their democratic credentials and distance themselves from China as a model. Kenyans,
on the contrary, could more easily toy with the idea of a "benevolent dictatorship."[11] As Hailemariam Desalegn – Ethiopia's Prime
Minister between 2012 and 2018 – explained, during his tenure as
chief whip of the EPRDF, Ethiopia's ruling party:

> We take some of the specific issues from different countries in
> different ways. [...] If you take the developmental bureaucracy,
> we take the Taiwanese. If you see democracy you cannot take the
> Chinese way. So there are different models you can take from
> different sectors of government. But we also say that we are a
> democratic developmental state, unlike the Asian Tigers in the
> beginning.[12]

As indicated by the excerpt opening this chapter, praises for the
Chinese government's forceful approach towards the media, and
ambition to turn them into a tool for economic development,
are not entirely absent. They are far from constituting, however,
a common trope in the discourses articulated by African leaders and politicians. As explained in the following chapter, when
introducing measures reducing freedom of expression online or
bolstering surveillance, governments have preferred to exploit the
contradictions of agendas promoted by Western donors, rather
than asserting their desire to follow the path charted by China.

China's *sovereign* Internet

A second, powerful narrative associated with the Chinese Internet has been rising in the past decade, this time with the spin and support of Chinese authorities, and in partial response to international criticism towards excessive censorship and control.

Six months after Hillary Clinton's "Remarks on Internet Freedom," when she condemned "countries [that] erected electronic barriers that prevent their people from accessing portions of the world's networks" and warned that "a new information curtain is descending across much of the world,"[13] the Chinese government released the first comprehensive manifesto detailing its own vision of the Internet. As Johan Lagerkvist noted, until then:

> There was no single cardinal document that specified an official ideology of what exactly the Chinese Internet should be about – apart from scattered, amorphous and hazy ideas of its being harmonious and protecting the psychology of the Chinese youth from overseas hostile values and forces.[14]

The document was launched as the "White Paper on the Internet *in* China," but its aim was to reach both domestic and foreign audiences. The core message for the United States, and any other country advocating the idea of one Internet, was built around the concept of a *sovereign* Internet. As the document made clear:

> The Internet sovereignty of China should be respected and protected. Citizens of the People's Republic of China and foreign citizens, legal persons and other organizations within Chinese territory have the right and freedom to use the Internet; at the same time, they must obey the laws and regulations of China and conscientiously protect Internet security.[15]

The White Paper was not exclusively aimed at stressing the Chinese government's right to build its own version of the Internet. It was also informed by the ambition of initiating a broader process to legitimize a new Internet doctrine, one that, shared by other countries, could make the Chinese case less exceptional. As the document stressed, broadening the focus beyond China:

"Though connected, the Internet of various countries belongs to different sovereignties." The importance of respecting distinctions among countries, and their political and cultural institutions, was made even clearer when addressing particularly sensitive issues, including Internet security:

> National situations and cultural traditions differ among countries, and so concern about Internet security also differs. Concerns about Internet security of different countries should be fully respected. We should seek common ground and reserve differences, promote development through exchanges, and jointly protect international Internet security.[16]

As pointed out by the China Rights Forum – a Chinese NGO seeking to promote awareness on the status of fundamental rights and freedoms in China – alongside a "made-for-export narrative," the process leading to the White Paper also produced an "internal narrative," where the Chinese party's Internet ideology was more fully articulated. When initially shared within China, however, some elements of this internal narrative – centered around the need for a "scientific, healthy, and orderly development of the Internet" – appeared too controversial even for Chinese audiences used to their government's tendency to take the upper hand in shaping the future of the national Internet. A report presented a few months before the White Paper by Wang Chen, the head of the Information Office of the State Council, titled "Concerning the Development and Management of Our Country's Internet," was first published online – exclusively in Chinese – but then removed a few days later, to be replaced by a new version with numerous sections omitted. Among those deleted were sections offering a blunter perspective on Internet sovereignty:

> The causes of problems online are extremely complex. Judging from the technological characteristics of the Internet, the Internet is a global open-information system. As long as our country's Internet is linked to the global Internet, there will be channels and means for all sorts of harmful foreign information to appear on our domestic Internet. [...] Judging

from our country's social development, our country is currently in a period of social transformation, rapid development, and conspicuous contradictions. Unavoidably, actual contradictions and problems in our society are reported on the Internet. Judging from our country's Internet management practices, we are still in the process of exploration and improvement. Many weak links still exist in our work. These problems have weakened our ability to manage the Internet scientifically and effectively.[17]

Statements such as these, as well as the whole incident around the report published online, offer an indication of the Chinese government's tendency to promote new policies and projects through trial and error, and progressive adjustments. As Jinghan Zeng, Tim Stevens, and Yaru Chen pointed out, seeking to unpack the domestic discourse of Internet sovereignty:

> The origins, meaning, and implementation of Internet sovereignty are sufficiently contested that much conceptual development is still required. [...] This is principally due to the evolving pattern of policy formation in China, whereby political ideas are often not clearly defined when first put forward by Chinese leaders.[18]

Shaping Internet norms

In this context, the White Paper on the Internet in China can be considered a starting point of a broader and more ambitious strategy aimed at progressively transforming China from a "norm-taker" to a "norm-shaper," and possibly a "norm-maker" in the long term,[19] a strategy significantly boosted since Xi Jinping became president in 2012, and which has been charted along two distinct, but related, trajectories.

A first component of this strategy has consisted in the Chinese government's increasingly decisive participation in debates and fora on Internet governance. Representation at the Internet Engineering Task Force (IETF) – the institution mandated to produce technical documents and standards related to the design, use, and management of the Internet – has been dramatically stepped up. As Nigel Inkster reported, in 2015 China sent 40 delegates to the IETF meeting, while most other countries sent just one or two.[20] After interrupting its participation in the consultations of the International Corporation of Assigned Names and Numbers (ICANN) – possibly the most critical institution regulating the global Internet, because of its control of Internet namespaces and the DNS root zone – in 2001 China sent again a delegate in 2009, marking the beginning of its re-engagement.[21]

The increased participation in Internet governance venues, while signaling greater interest and capacity to influence technical decisions, also constitutes a powerful message on changing balances of power. As a member of the African Internet Society (ISOC) who is a regular attendee of Internet governance conferences remarked, comparing the American and Chinese participation in the World Telecommunication Development Conference in Buenos Aires in 2017:

> The US used to have so many resources to dominate these spaces, but it seems they have their own internal problems now. Many in Buenos Aires noticed that the US delegation was not prepared, while the Chinese sent very bright minds. If it continues like this, their domination is likely to increase.[22]

This new phase of international exposure in charting the future of the global Internet, while marked by greater assertiveness and arguably more constructive tones when compared to the 2000s,[23] has also maintained continuity with the past. Above all, great emphasis has continued to be placed on the need to shift from the multi-stakeholder approach favored by the United States since the beginning of consultations on the global Internet to a multilateral approach to Internet governance. As clearly articulated by Lu Wei, the first powerful director of the Cyberspace Administration of China – the agency created in 2014 to offer central control and oversight to the Chinese Internet – in an editorial for the *Huffington Post* titled "Cyber Sovereignty Must Rule Global Internet":

> With regard to the cyberspace governance, the U.S. advocates "multi-stakeholders" while China believes in "multi-lateral." ["Multi-stakeholder" refers to all Internet participants on

an equal footing making the rules and is considered more "people-centered" while "multi-lateral" refers to the state making the rules based on the ideas of the sovereignty of the nation-state representing its citizens.][24]

The tension between multi-stakeholderism and multilateralism broke out in the open during the 2012 World Conference on International Telecommunications (WCIT), organized by the International Telecommunication Union (ITU) in Dubai to update and revise the International Telecommunication Regulations (ITRs). The conference, in principle, was aimed at discussing relatively technical aspects for the interoperability of telecommunications, but was transformed into a highly political affair on the nature and future of the Internet. Countries proposing a greater mandate for the ITU, a multilateral institution, and more powers to national governments were accused of trying to fragment the Internet. Campaigns and petitions were organized by international advocacy groups to warn them, China and Russia above all, to keep their "hands off our Internet."[25] In the opposite camp, the nations defending the idea of one Internet and multi-stakeholderism were accused to be protecting the privileged position they had acquired as early adopters of the Internet and limit possibilities for latecomers to contribute to the shaping of national and global information societies. In an unusual turn for an international conference of the kind of the WCIT, normally ending with consensus on a negotiated document, 55 nations, most of them liberal democracies, voted against the new ITRs, while another 87 signed the updated regulations.

The second component of the strategy pursued by the Chinese government to assert its vision of a sovereign Internet, rather than visibly articulating an alternative in international fora still dominated by the idea of one Internet, has consisted in consolidating parallel venues of like-minded states sharing similar conceptions of the future of the Internet. The most notable initiative originated in the context of the Shanghai Cooperation Organization (SCO), a forum established in 2001 to explore normative and legal consensus around security threats such as

terrorism, separatism, and extremism in Eurasia. (The found-
ing members were China, Kazakhstan, Kyrgyzstan, Russia,
Tajikistan, and Uzbekistan; India and Pakistan joined in 2017.)
In 2011, China, Russia, Tajikistan, and Uzbekistan elaborated a
document – the "International Code of Conduct for Information
Security" – detailing their vision for a set of standards that could
be applied globally to regulate the protection of national information spaces and persecute those seeking to penetrate into
national information and network infrastructure. The document
was submitted to the UN General Assembly first in 2011, and
then again in 2015, in a revised form, with the extended support
of Kazakhstan and Kyrgyzstan. The second submission sought
to capitalize on the changed international environment emerged
from Edward Snowden's revelations in 2013, offering evidence
of a more malicious approach towards breaches to security and
privacy adopted by the United States on a global scale. The documents reaffirmed, once again, the idea of a sovereign Internet,
stressing that "policy authority for Internet-related public issues
is the sovereign right of States."[26]

Another key venue to collectively advance the ideal of a sovereign Internet was created by the Cyberspace Administration of
China in 2014 in Wuzhen, a historic town near Hangzhou, home
to the headquarters of e-commerce giant Alibaba. Dubbed the
"World Internet Conference" (WIC), the event hosted heads of
state and Internet companies to promote conversations on the
future of the Internet that could stand in alternative to those
emerging from other venues, such as the "London Conference,"
a series of gatherings created to stand midway between multilateralism and multi-stakeholderism and "propagate the values and
ideals of an open and global cyberspace."[27] In 2015, the WIC was
opened by President Xi Jinping, who used assertive tones to elaborate on the Chinese government's Internet doctrine. He made clear
that "no country should pursue cyber hegemony, interfere in other
countries' internal affairs or engage in, connive at or support cyber
activities that undermine other countries' national security," and
that all should "respect the right of individual countries to independently choose their own path of cyber development, model of

cyber regulation and Internet public policies, and participate in international cyberspace governance on an equal footing".[28]

China's more assertive foreign policy of the Internet is ambitious and may aspire to progressively chart a new Internet doctrine, but to date has been confined to a relatively limited set of like-minded countries in China's most immediate geographical sphere of influence and has had some limited successes in international fora. As discussed in more detail below, African countries appear to have not been directly targeted or engaged to build a common front advocating for a different, sovereign, idea of the Internet. Issues related to cybercrime and cybersecurity have been placed on the agenda of professional associations such as the Asian–African Legal Consultative Organization (AALCO), seeking to explain the merits of a UN-centric approach to Internet governance, but to date there are no signs of larger, more concerted efforts to take this agenda to Africa.

China's Internet

The narratives on China's *censored* and *sovereign* Internet represent complementary attempts to characterize, externally and internally, and simplify – mostly for external consumption – the complex system that has emerged around ICTs in a vast and diverse country.

They rely on and magnify aspects that do belong to China's emergent information society – the attempt of the government to contain and control dissent as well as the aspiration of tweaking ICTs in ways that more closely resonate with China's distinctive technological and political trajectories – but also obscure important phenomena that have uniquely emerged within China. These narratives emphasize the importance of the state while downplaying the role users have played in shaping online communication, and are far from offering a comprehensive picture of what the Chinese Internet actually looks like.

While it makes little sense to try to capture a supposed essence of a China's information society, recent academic literature has made tremendous progress in offering a more nuanced picture of what life online is like in China. To be sure, the first wave of studies on the Internet in China was driven by concerns that are remarkably similar to those expressed in the policy realm. As the authors of one of the first systematic analysis of early academic debates concluded: "The overwhelming bulk of published research on China's Internet seeks to answer just two questions: Can China build an Internet, and if so, can China control it?"[29] It is only in the past decade that studies accounting for the complexities of the Chinese Internet have begun to emerge, moving beyond the preoccupations with access and control, and offering a fuller picture of the role the Internet has been playing in the Chinese society.

Negotiating spaces for expression and charting new paths for influence

The Chinese Internet has been shaped by a complex and ever-changing web of negotiations between users, Internet intermediaries (e.g. Internet service providers, social networking platforms), traditional media, and public authorities, which, while ensuring overall stability is not threatened, allows even substantial transformations to occur. Rebecca MacKinnon, drawing inspiration from a provocation by novelist and blogger Yang Hengjun, suggested looking at the Internet in China as a "special political zone," emerging in the footsteps of the "special economic zones" created by Deng Xiaoping to test more liberal economic policies with smaller populations.[30] The Internet has become a space for experimentation, for users and authorities to test each other out, for some to speak and others to listen, and in some cases to act upon what they heard. In this zone, there is no certainty, but, differently from other spaces dominated by an authoritarian logic, there is a sense of opportunity that voice may shape decisions and policies.

A plethora of studies have been tracing how online uproars have forced authorities to change their course of action, even in dramatic ways, and some of these cases have come to represent landmarks in the evolution of online participation in China.[31]

The death in police custody of 27-year-old Sun Zhigang is among the most significant and well reported. Yuezhi Zhao has offered probably the most comprehensive account of this incident, locating Sun's death in the context of the growth in complexity and diversification of China's media system, as well as in relation to the discrimination suffered by Chinese migrants moving from rural to urban centers. As she wrote: "Sun was born in a poor village, but he managed to cross the rural/urban divide by passing the university entrance exam, thus acquiring urban citizenship status. [...] He became the first person in his village since 1949 to gain urban citizenship." Once he moved to Guangzhou, while still waiting for his residence permit, Sun was rounded up in a raid organized against vagrants forbidden to live in urban centers. After his arrest, "Sun was singled out for corporal punishment because he protested and resisted his treatment," trying to explain his case. He died the next day, beaten up by his inmates, who were told by police they were free to "play around" with him.[32]

Sun's death was initially covered by silence. His family lacked the means and networks to bring the case to the attention of the authorities or the media. Only when Sun's classmates reached the *Nanfang Metropolitan News* (NMS), a progressive newspaper targeting working- and middle-class readers in Guandong, and when the paper chose to publish an investigative report revealing details about Sun's death, the story gained first local and then national attention. The two-page article in NMS initiated a seemingly unstoppable wave. Shared on the Internet, the news spread across the country and caused national indignation. Other papers began reporting on the case, and when NMS's follow-up story was killed by censors, it found its way onto the Internet: "The impact of the mobilization was immediate. 23 officials [...] received disciplinary actions – eight police chiefs and officers [...] were fired."[33] Soon after, Premier Wen Jiabao signed a new law that not only abolished previous measures against rural migrants, but also launched new welfare programs to assist them in cities.

Sun's case is only one of many that challenge the simplistic rhetoric of censorship and control that dominates discourses and perceptions surrounding the Chinese Internet. Within the Great Firewall, myriad interactions occur with the potential to lead to concrete outcomes. As the government's decision to radically change approach towards Chinese internal migrants shows, some of these outcomes may even go beyond what online mobilizations are able to achieve in more open regimes.

The government strikes back

Despite the increasing occurrence and significance of online uproars, there have been many cases in which public authorities have failed or refused to act on users' demands.[34] And there have also been many attempts to prevent some of these interactions from reaching a critical mass.[35] The attack led by Lu Wei – the disgraced but once powerful director of the Cyberspace Administration of China – against China's Big Vs is probably one of the most dramatic examples of the ability of the state to respond to threats emerging from online communication. The term Big V refers to the verified users of the microblogging service Weibo with a very large follower base. Similar to Twitter, since its launch in 2009 Sina Weibo has offered to its users the opportunity to broadcast views and opinions to increasingly large audiences, following communicative dynamics that progressively challenged the ability of centralized power to control and shape communication. As Rogier Creemers reported, the response to this threat was particularly severe.[36] First, "a People's Daily editorial on 26 August 2013 stated that 'Big Vs' must not become 'Big Rumours.'"[37] This marked the beginning of the clampdown on some of China's most vocal Big Vs:

> On 30 August, the American–Chinese businessman Charles Xue (or Xue Manzi), a Big V with 12 million followers, was arrested and publicly pilloried on CCTV. While he was officially charged with solicitation, his detention was widely seen as retaliation for his online behaviour.[38]

His public shaming attracted both national and international attention, but he was not the only Big V to be targeted to offer tangible examples to other users: "Two other online culprits, nicknamed Qin Huohuo and Li'erchaisi were accused of mobilizing an 'Internet Water Army', which flooded social media with false information, often for commercial gain."[39]

While these events set the tone of the campaign, they were later followed by policies aimed at institutionalizing and legitimizing measures against the influence of Big Vs. If a post was found to contain false information and was either rebroadcast 500 times or viewed 5,000 times, it could land its author to up to three years in prison. One of the first consequences of this move was a significant exodus to other services, such as WeChat, which, similarly to WhatsApp, facilitated more private forms of communication among users and within smaller groups.[40]

The relationship between online users and public authorities should not be understood, however, only in antagonistic terms, with users on one side seeking to force institutions to respond and change, and the state apparatus on the other seeking to constrain and silence demands from below. As Johan Lagerkvist explained through a detailed analysis of scandals and online mobilizations, new propaganda tactics have evolved to enlist online users in operations aimed – ostensively – at bringing transparency on the very actions of the state and its institutions.[41] A notable example of this strategy was the response to the death of an inmate in a detention center in Kunming, the capital of Yunnan Province, in 2009. Soon after the incident, unconvinced with the official explanations provided by local authorities, bloggers and online activists mounted an online campaign demanding the truth was publicly revealed. Rather than shutting them down, the vice-director of the local propaganda department asked activists to join an investigative team that would collectively look into the matter. While the team did not uncover evidence that significantly challenged the earlier verdict, this move progressively led to the fading of online mobilizations and debates around the incident.[42]

Cases such as these illustrate the new pragmatism that has progressively emerged among China's political elites, which has characterized not only online uproars demanding transparency and accountability, but also other forms of online expressions, from belligerent calls to action from Chinese nationalists, who both threaten and support the hegemony of the CCP,[43] to middle-class pressures for greater respect for the environment.[44]

From control to authoritarian deliberation

Research mapping these types of negotiations – forcing authorities to take action, leading to crackdowns on users, or connecting users and public authorities in the pursuit of a shared objective – has become more readily available, but it is still difficult to capture what separates successful from unsuccessful demands. As Jonathan Hassid has argued, the regime of uncertainty that has come to characterize China's media system is instrumental for the exercise of state power and control, and for encouraging self-censorship.[45]

This does not mean that the outcomes of the negotiations with power that are taking place online are arbitrary. Analyzing more broadly how public authorities in China have responded to citizen demands, Baogang He and Mark Warren have suggested using the concept of *authoritarian deliberation* to capture the mechanisms through which the Chinese state has allowed political change to occur in the absence of democratic institutions.[46] The concept, they admit, rests on a paradox, but it is at the same time "conceptually possible, empirically existent, and functionally motivated." The development of theories of democracy and deliberation has been closely intertwined, but this does not mean that linkages between democracy and deliberation are necessary. "Deliberation is a mode of communication in which participants in a political process offer and respond to the substance of claims, reasons, and perspectives in ways that generate persuasion-based influence."[47] Also, in the absence of democratic institutions, this influence may lead to concrete outcomes, if elites have incentives to recognize it, seeking, for example, to maintain or increase their legitimacy.

Among the explanations offered to why a form of authoritarian deliberation has emerged in China, He and Warren have stressed, in particular, the ability of deliberative mechanisms to "co-opt dissent and maintain social order." Adopting Hirschman's typology of exit, voice, and loyalty, they have argued that:

The Chinese Communist Party (CCP) faces functional limits in two of the three means of controlling dissent. Currently, the CCP controls high profile political dissent with an exit strategy, allowing dissidents to immigrate to the US and other countries to minimize their domestic impact. Internally, the CCP buys the loyalty of party members with senior positions, privileges, and grants. But simply owing to their numbers, neither strategy can be applied to the hundreds of millions of ordinary Chinese, who are quite capable of collective forms of dissent. Suppression is always possible and often used selectively against internal dissidents. But like all overtly coercive tactics, overuse produces diminishing returns. In the case of China, suppression risks undermining the increasing openness that supports its development agenda, as well as generating international attention that may also have economic consequences. Thus voice is the remaining option for controlling dissent and maintaining order. The CCP has for some time pursued a policy of channeling dissent onto a developing court system, as well as into low level elections. But CCP officials are discovering, often through trial and error, that regular and frequent deliberative meetings can reduce dissent, social conflict and complaints, while saving money, personnel, and time.[48]

The concept of authoritarian deliberation has not been elaborated to capture the negotiations between citizens and public authorities that are occurring online, but broader changes that have occurred at the level of state–society relations in China. Its relevance and implications for the Internet, however, as a space allowing constant, real-time, and traceable deliberations, as well as learning through trial and error, are clear. Numerous scholars have adopted it to explain essential features that have come to characterize China's information society.[49] For those willing to explore whether and how the Internet has changed power dynamics in China, beyond the simplistic – albeit not inaccurate – perception of surveillance and control, authoritarian deliberation offers the closest approximation to what a Chinese model of the "political" Internet may look like.

Communicating the Chinese Internet

Bringing the perspective back to Africa, how has China related to these narratives when interacting with African actors? As hinted above, referring to a supposedly coherent Chinese "model" of the Internet, or magnifying one aspect over others, can be misleading. China has responded very differently to different discourses on its emergent information society and its possible global ramifications.

The following sections seek to analyze and compare how these responses have been articulated, focusing on key spaces where Chinese and African actors have come into contact when considering different ideas of the information society, or concretely implementing projects on the ground: Chinese media targeting African audiences; global and regional forums debating Internet governance; academic scholarship; and technical projects connecting Chinese and African actors operating in the ICT sector.

Chinese media in Africa: a notable silence

Given the unprecedented efforts to boost China's media presence in Africa, it would be legitimate to expect the Chinese government to make use of its international broadcasters, news agencies, and global editions of its newspapers to also shape narratives on what China's media system is actually like and support its normative agenda on ICTs. To date, however, this has happened to a very limited extent.

In 2012, China Central Television (CCTV) launched CCTV Africa, its production center in Nairobi and the largest operation of a foreign TV broadcaster on African soil. Adding to an already strengthened African arm of Xinhua, China's official press agency, CCTV Africa (later rebranded China Global Television Network – CGTN) had a very ambitious agenda. It purportedly aimed at changing narratives on Africa, placing renewed emphasis on the continent's achievements and opportunities. As Song Janing, CCTV Africa's first director, explained: "The other international media have advantages. They have been operating before us. We are very new. But we have our priorities and ideas. We hope to strengthen a positive image of Africa in Africa and worldwide."[50]

As the now increasingly abundant literature on CCTV/CGTN Africa illustrates, however, this goal has appeared more complex to achieve in practice, and a different strategy seems to have characterized CCTV/CGTN and other Chinese media operations on African soil. As suggested by Xiaoling Zhang's analysis of the programs produced by CCTV/CGTN Africa, Vivien Marsh's comparison of CCTV/CGTN's Africa Live and BBC's Focus on Africa, and Emeka Umejei's research on African journalists working for Chinese media in Africa, three trends appear to have shaped CCTV/CGTN Africa's reporting.[51] First, despite claims that Africa deserves to be better portrayed in international media, the majority of news items on Africa are either neutral or negative, and the tone does not appear dramatically different from its competitors. Second, it is when it comes to the West, and to the United States in particular, that CCTV/CGTN Africa appears more aggressive in putting forward alternative narratives, questioning the United States' behavior in Africa or some of the doctrines embraced by the United States – for example, highlighting links between elections and instability in Africa. Third, despite news on China or on Chinese initiatives in Africa being unsurprisingly positive, they come short of presenting China as a model to follow or advancing some of the strategies China has adopted for its own development as something Africa should learn from.

I have sought to explain the reasons for the mismatch between declared and enacted policies elsewhere,[52] but what is particularly relevant to remark here is how Chinese media have largely avoided a strategy aimed at changing perceptions of China directly. They have rather preferred to question the policies of some of China's adversaries, or to create new associations altogether – along the lines of the strategy Russia, another powerful nation contesting existing balances of power, has mastered to weaken the position of its adversaries, while concealing its own contradictions.[53] This choice partially depends on the intrinsic challenges of transforming negative perceptions. As linguist George Lakoff explained, if someone is told "Don't think of an elephant!" he will likely start "summoning the bulkiness, the grayness, the trunkiness of an elephant. [...] When we negate a frame, we evoke a frame."[54] This remark is particularly relevant in relation to the narrative on the Chinese Internet as a censored Internet. Given the widespread criticism surrounding media freedoms in China, news stories in Chinese media suggesting China is *not* how it is usually portrayed would likely be received with suspicion and possibly backfire.

A limited use of Chinese media in Africa has also been made to communicate or clarify China's more assertive stance towards a sovereign Internet. CCTV/CGTN Africa has regularly covered key events where alternative ideas of the Internet have been articulated, including the conference in Wuzhen, but rather than focusing on policy issues, its reporting has privileged highlighting the accomplishments of Chinese companies and entrepreneurs, spinning an image of China as an innovation powerhouse. Also in this case, Chinese media seem to have chosen to create new associations, rather than contesting old images and becoming entangled in controversial issues of Internet governance, where the United States' position on the global Internet appears still dominant, and China has only recently started to articulate its own.

International fora: a space for asserting a sovereign Internet?

The more sheltered venues of diplomatic gatherings seem to have offered a more comfortable space for Chinese politicians, diplomats, and technocrats to experiment and seek influencing global perceptions. Especially when it comes to the idea of a sovereign Internet, greater efforts have been made by the Chinese government to frame this conception as particularly appealing for developing countries and present China as seeking to advance not just its own, but also their, interests. As President Xi Jinping argued in his opening remarks of the 2015 Wuzhen conference:

> The information gap between different countries and regions is widening, and the existing rules governing the cyberspace hardly reflect the desires and interests of the majority of countries. [...] China stands ready to work with all parties concerned to come up with more investment and technical support to jointly advance the building of global Internet infrastructure and enable more developing countries and their people to share the development opportunities brought by the Internet.[55]

This position has been further amplified and articulated by Chinese diplomats and think tanks. The China Institute of International Studies, commenting on Xi's remarks, added: "As the largest developing country, China needs to express its views in face of global challenges as it can reflect the interests of other developing countries, bringing equity and justice to international governance."[56] Similarly, an article published by the Institute for Security & Development Studies sought to frame the position of developing countries as supposedly more favorable towards China's pledge for a sovereign Internet. As its author argued:

> The "multi-stakeholder" model is often framed as a bottom-up policy process that encompasses a range of actors from governments, businesses, technical experts, and civil society. However, this model is often seen by other countries, especially emerging powers as well as developing countries, as one which favors the economic and security interests of the U.S. They instead advocate that actors participate in the IG process on a more equal footing. In particular they argue for the greater involvement of multilateral organizations, such as the ITU as a UN agency, in which governments play the primary role in public policymaking related to IG.[57]

Despite the investment in presenting the idea of sovereign Internets as appealing for developing countries, it is important to stress the specificity of this discourse. The insistence on sovereignty has become an essential feature of Chinese domestic and foreign policy, but does not account to offering China as a model. Sovereignty is not a substantive discourse, one that incorporates indications of the specific ways in which national information societies should be shaped. Rather, it aims at creating a space for each national polity to find its unique combination of technologies, actors, and discourses in the developing of its own path towards development.

Similar to what has been the case in other venues for international politics, also in the case of Internet governance, China has been reluctant to portray itself as a model others should follow. Those attending public events on international development listing Chinese diplomats and development experts among their speakers have become acquainted with the insistence that China does not have ready-made lessons for Africa. In the case of some diplomats and government officials, this attitude may appear an excessive – almost unnatural – display of modesty, hiding, on the contrary, a sense of confidence and superiority, but it continues to represent the official position when interacting with foreign partners or competitors, seeking to contain perceptions of China emerging as a hegemonic power, imposing its doctrine on others.

China's Internet: unfit for export?

As mentioned earlier, academic literature has played a paramount role in developing a more nuanced understanding of the Chinese Internet as a contested space for experimentation. Despite evidence of the unique features of China's information society becoming more readily available, however, the Chinese government seems to have done very little to build on it, sharing strategies and lessons that could be followed by other countries.

Arguably, many of the elements that characterize the negotiations occurring between citizens and the state described above rest on a unique mix of factors that have come to define power relations in contemporary China, which is unlikely to emerge in other contexts. The absence of national elections as a mechanism for political expression, the high-modernist project embraced by the Communist Party, the progressive ascension to the status of global power, the availability of a large base of educated youth, are all elements that are difficult to find elsewhere, and in the same combination. Despite the Communist Party's emphasis on forward planning, many of the mechanisms regulating the balance between grassroots demands and political change have emerged as unprompted responses to a fast-changing sociotechnical reality. Some of these mechanisms may have become more recognizable and relatively institutionalized over time, but they cannot be easily replicated elsewhere or proposed as a solution to the challenges faced by other national polities.

As scholar Li Zhibiao pointed out, reflecting on China's development path more broadly, and its significance for Africa:

If African nations really want to study and learn from the Chinese experience, first, they must thoroughly understand the differences and similarities between their national situation and that of China. Second, they must research in earnest all of the aspects of China's, and even other countries', developmental experience, and moreover, on the basis of that, search for the developmental strategy and road that contains the characteristics [most appropriate for] themselves.[58]

A niche of African scholars, experts, and politicians seem to have embarked on a process of the kind Li describes, developing deeper understandings of the traits characterizing China's information societies and the (im)possibility to replicate them in African contexts. As Daniel Berhane, one of Ethiopia's most vocal bloggers, exemplified, answering a question about whether Ethiopia is taking cues from China, especially when it comes to using online spaces for gauging public opinion and possibly acting on emerging demands:

I know of cases when I wrote something and the Ethiopian government took note. So they accept indications if they are properly delivered. If they see it as constructive criticism they may accept it. But there is a lot of stuff there that is not written for this reason. And if it does not convince me, why should it convince the Prime Minister? In Ethiopia it is not the Chinese model that they try to emulate. In Ethiopia the system is polarized. If this government accepts some changes in no way it will let its critics take credit for it. And in any case things are framed in a way that discourages the government to take note.[59]

As Daniel's words suggest, a deeper understanding of the functioning of China's "special political zones," to return to MacKinnon's definition, does not imply a desire to try to replicate their dynamics. Even when this understanding is marked by a sense of admiration for China, as expressed by Sebhat Nega at the beginning of this chapter, it is often accompanied by the awareness of the complexities that would be encountered trying to emulate it in a different sociopolitical context.

Transfer failure

If we shift the focus away from the complex web of interactions characterizing China's "political" Internet and its relevance for Africa, to other, more discrete elements that have characterized the evolution of the Internet in China, the reluctance to offer lessons for Africa appears more puzzling.

Many of the Ethiopian, Kenyan, and Ghanaian engineers and computer scientists I interviewed who had worked with Chinese counterparts often seemed surprised by their colleagues' lack of interest in applying or transferring lessons that had characterized the evolution of ICTs in China. In this case, they were not referring to a supposedly coherent model of the information society, but to policy and technical solutions that had helped China's ICT market to grow.

In its own path towards development, China has demonstrated a remarkable ability to localize foreign technologies and utilize aid and foreign direct investment to strengthen its domestic market and industries.[60] The insistence on a no-strings-attached approach and the tendency to privilege turnkey projects, however, has created few opportunities for knowledge transfer and for some of the strategies China has progressively developed, often through trial and error, to be transferred to its African partners. This determination goes so far that the support to the expanding access to mobile phones and the Internet under monopoly in Ethiopia, for example, has gone against the very experience China acquired in expanding its own telecommunication system.

China's transition from a socialist regime that emphasized monopoly to an increasingly liberalized market, under internal and external pressures to reform – the latter particularly tied to the process of accessing the WTO – could have offered important lessons for Ethiopia. China's path towards liberalization was initially marred by failed attempts to open up and by power struggles between different ministries, but eventually led to the creation of the largest market of mobile and Internet users in the world.[61] The Chinese government began this process by first allowing limited forms of competition among companies still closely tied to central power, and then progressively opening to foreign direct investments. Rather than shaking the market with a sector reform that would have potentially led to uncontrollable transformations, smaller changes were introduced, tested, and in some cases reversed.[62] This sequence of trial and error is far from a textbook approach to liberalization, but could have offered an important base from which to develop targeted measures for opening up the Ethiopian telecommunication system, also characterized by a socialist emphasis on monopoly and resistance to the changes a sudden liberalization might lead to. This point was even recognized by Chinese experts working in the telecommunications sector in Africa. As a representative of Huawei remarked:

> Ethiopia should open up and allow more competition in the market if it wants to achieve its goals. Ethio Telecom, because of its poor standing, is too afraid that if anybody comes in the market all customers will go to the new company and Ethio Telecom will not survive ... Working with governments that are too centralized is frustrating because they slow things down a lot, as there is not urgency in responding to their competitors.[63]

Keeping the monopoly and entrusting all expansion projects to one company led to the creation of a poorly functioning system with little incentive to improve itself. This ultimately affected the reputation of ETC/Ethio Telecom and of ZTE itself, to the point that even tightly controlled official government media in Ethiopia, including *Addis Zemen* and the *Ethiopian Herald*, have been allowed to criticize technical glitches and incompetence. Even staff at ETC/Ethio Telecom recognized that cooperation with ZTE came as a mixed bag. As a mid-level manager conceded:

> There has not been a great transfer of knowledge. The Chinese work alone. Especially at the beginning there were many problems. The Chinese were doing everything on their own. And we realized that this was risky. They had all the privileges over the network. So over time we changed and now we are in control. And we can ask them to help us on specific things. But there is still dependency.[64]

Another ICT specialist, who has been involved in numerous government-led ICT projects in Ethiopia, summarized the relationship between the Chinese and the Ethiopian companies by suggesting that "they are experimenting on us, but in the end we are getting the services that we need."[65] He also noted, however, that when checks and balances are absent or too few, this experimentation may leave all parties worse off in the end. Referring to the delays in signing contracts with ZTE and Huawei after they had won the 2011 tender, he argued:

> It is about politics. We are a one-party system. There are internal issues and power struggles. It is more about power than about finding the right solutions for the problems that we face.
> Different politicians have different interests. Before with Meles there was a greater sense of urgency. If something needed to be done, it was done. He would step in and give direction. This is lacking now.[66]

Even Huawei publicly expressed frustration at the slow pace at which the Ethiopian government was making decisions.[67] This, however, did not lead the company to challenge the model Ethiopia had envisioned or try to steer it in different directions. Despite some of Huawei's representatives believing that competition would have actually helped the Ethiopian government in reaching its goals, these remained just personal opinions.

This is an example of how China's resistance to interfering in domestic affairs may ultimately backfire. Paradoxically perhaps, Chinese companies have fared better in countries where they have been operating in a regime of tougher competition, as has been the case in China since the early 2000s. As explained earlier, in neighboring Kenya, Huawei has been contracted not just as part of vendor financing packages, as in the case of Ethiopia; it has also won contracts with private operators because of its ability to offer good value for money.[68]

In Ethiopia, on the contrary, the lack of pressure to beat competitors and the limited checks and balances have created a dangerous space where no partner has had incentives to improve the system to higher standards, ultimately leaving the citizens, whose life the Ethiopian government has affirmed it wants to improve through ICTs, worse off than in other countries where the state has invested much less in new communication technologies.

Conclusion

Most scholars are well aware that when talking about China–Africa – or Africa–China – they oversimplify and risk obfuscating a reality that is complex, multifaceted, and often contradictory. Novelists and experts have joked about popular perceptions of Africa as a country.[69] And even if China is a country, its vastness and rapid changes should warn analysts seeking to capture trends that are unitary and definite.

This chapter has sought to account for some of this complexity, when it comes to ideas about China's information society, both as emerging from China itself, or as part of processes of thinking, talking and writing about China from the outside. Even analyses and narrations that account for more nuanced understandings of the complex relationships that have emerged online between Chinese citizens and public authorities, and appear as more realistic descriptions of the Chinese Internet, can be challenged by rapid changes in policy. An example are the limitations on Internet freedom progressively introduced by Xi Jinping, seeking to erode some of the spaces for experimentations emerged during the tenure of his predecessors.[70]

When analyzing China–Africa relations in the information sector, it is thus important not only to identify which actors are entering into a relationship – as discussed in the previous chapter – but also what the direction of this relationship is. If China is not trying to advocate a particular model, are there any attempts from African partners to copy elements that have guided the evolution of the Internet in China? And if so, how detailed, and current, is the understanding of these elements? Or, rather than trying to copy a strategy, is there anything unique emerging from the combination of different technologies, discourses, and actors that does not have equivalents elsewhere?

Notes

1 US Embassy in Addis Ababa, "Wikileaks Cable #09ADDISABABA149," 2009.

2 Interview: Sebhat Nega, Founder of the TPLF and Director of the Ethiopian International Institute for Peace & Development. Addis Ababa, May 11, 2013.

3 Zimbabwe's ousted president Robert Mugabe is among the few African heads of state who publicly declared the need for African governments to learn from China how to shape their national information societies. See Kabweza, "Chinese Style Internet Censorship Coming to Zimbabwe – President Mugabe."

4 Benjamin Haas, "China Moves to Block Internet VPNs from 2018," *The Guardian*, July 11, 2017, www. theguardian.com/world/2017/jul/11/ china-moves-to-block-internet-vpns-from-2018.

5 Reporters Without Borders, "China: World's Leading Prison for Citizen Journalists," 2017, https://rsf. org/en/china.

6 Reporters Without Borders, "Enemies of the Internet," 2014, http://12mars.rsf.org/2014-en/.

7 Wang in Mark Leonard, *What Does China Think?* (Fourth Estate, 2008), 76.

8 Pew Research Center, "Global Indicators Database," *Pew Research Center's Global Attitudes Project*, 2017, www.pewglobal.org/database/.

9 Interview: David Newton, Rector, Ghana's Institute of Journalism. Accra, Ghana, August 26, 2010.

10 Interview: Samuel Okudzeto Ablakwa, Deputy Minister of Information. Accra, Ghana, August 24, 2010.

11 Elsje Fourie, *New Maps for Africa? Contextualising the "Chinese Model" within Ethiopian and Kenyan Paradigms of Development* (University of Trento, 2013).

12 Quoted in Fourie, *New Maps for Africa?* 332–333.

13 Clinton, "Remarks on Internet Freedom."

14 Johan Lagerkvist, *After the Internet, before Democracy: Competing Norms in Chinese Media and Society* (Peter Lang, 2010), 61–62.

15 State Council of the People's Republic of China, "The Internet in China. White Paper," June 8, 2010, www.china.org.cn/government/ whitepaper/node_7093508.htm.

16 State Council of the People's Republic of China, "The Internet in China. White Paper," June 8, 2010, www.china.org.cn/government/ whitepaper/node_7093508.htm

17 C. Wang, "Concerning the Development and Administration of Our Country's Internet," *China Rights Forum* 2 (2010), www.hrichina.org/en/ content/3241.

18 Jinghan Zeng, Tim Stevens, and Yaru Chen, "China's Solution to Global Cyber Governance: Unpacking the Domestic Discourse of 'Internet Sovereignty,'" *Politics & Policy* 45, no. 3 (2017): 446.

19 Zeng, Stevens, and Chen, "China's Solution to Global Cyber

Governance"; Jinghan Zeng and Shaun Breslin, "China's 'New Type of Great Power Relations': A G2 with Chinese Characteristics?" *International Affairs* 92, no. 4 (2016): 773–794.

20 Nigel Inkster, "Battle for the Soul of the Internet," *Adelphi Series* 55, no. 456 (2015): 109–142.

21 Hong Shen, "China and Global Internet Governance: Toward an Alternative Analytical Framework," *Chinese Journal of Communication* 9, no. 3 (July 2, 2016): 304–324, https:// doi.org/10.1080/17544750.2016. 1206028.

22 Interview: Verengai Mabika, Internet Society. Johannesburg, South Africa, January 11, 2018.

23 Séverine Arsène, "Global Internet Governance in Chinese Academic Literature: Rebalancing a Hegemonic World Order?" *China Perspectives*, no. 2 (2016): 25.

24 Lu Wei, "Cyber Sovereignty Must Rule Global Internet," *Huffington Post*, December 15, 2014, www.huffingtonpost.com/lu-wei/ china-cyber-sovereignty_b_6324060. html.

25 AVAAZ, "Click Here to Save the Free Internet!" *AVAAZ*, 2012, https://secure.avaaz.org/en/hands_ off_our_internet_i/.

26 Sarah McKune, "Analysis of International Code of Conduct," *The Citizen Lab*, September 28, 2015, https://citizenlab.ca/2015/09/ international-code-of-conduct/.

27 Samuel Cherian, "Asian Participation in the London Process," *Institute for Defence*

Studies and Analyses, March 31, 2015, https://idsa.in/idsacomments/ AsianParticipationintheLondon Process%2520_csamuel_310315.

28 Xi Jinping, "Remarks by H.E. Xi Jinping President of the People's Republic of China at the Opening Ceremony of the Second World Internet Conference," *Ministry of Foreign Affairs of the People's Republic of China*, 2015, www.fmprc. gov.cn/mfa_eng/wjdt_665385/ zyjh_665391/t1327570.shtml.

29 Randolph Kluver and Chen Yang, "The Internet in China: A Meta-Review of Research," *The Information Society* 21, no. 4 (2005): 301–308.

30 Rebecca MacKinnon, "Cyber Zone," *Index on Censorship* 37, no. 2 (2008): 82–89.

31 See, for example, Jack Linchuan Qiu and Wei Bu, "China ICT Studies: A Review of the Field, 1989–2012," *China Review* 13, no. 2 (2013): 123–152; Jack Linchuan Qiu, "Goodbye ISlave: Foxconn, Digital Capitalism, and Networked Labor Resistance," *Society: Chinese Journal of Sociology/ Shehui* 34, no. 4 (2014); Lokman Tsui, "An Inadequate Metaphor: The Great Firewall and Chinese Internet Censorship," *Global Dialogue* 9, no. 1/2 (2007): 60; Lokman Tsui, "Internet Opening up China: Fact or Fiction," in *Media in Transition: Globalization & Convergence Conference* (MIT Press, 2002), 10–12; MacKinnon, "Cyber Zone"; Rogier Creemers, "Cyber China: Upgrading Propaganda, Public Opinion Work and Social Management for the Twenty-First

Century," *Journal of Contemporary China*, 26, no. 103 (2017): 85–100; Yuezhi Zhao, *Communication in China: Political Economy, Power, and Conflict* (Rowman & Littlefield, 2008); Yuezhi Zhao, "Understanding China's Media System in a World Historical Context," *Comparing Media Systems beyond the Western World*, 2012, 143–173; Guobin Yang, *The Power of the Internet in China: Citizen Activism Online* (Columbia University Press, 2013).

32 Zhao, *Communication in China*.

33 Zhao, *Communication in China*.

34 Anne SY Cheung, "Exercising Freedom of Speech behind the Great Firewall: A Study of Judges' and Lawyers' Blogs in China," *Harvard International Law Journal Online* 52, no. 250 (2011), http://papers.ssrn.com/sol3/papers.cfm?abstract_id=1844003.

35 Gary King, Jennifer Pan, and Margaret E. Roberts, "How Censorship in China Allows Government Criticism but Silences Collective Expression," *American Political Science Review* 107, no. 2 (2013): 326–343.

36 Creemers, "Cyber China."

37 Creemers, "Cyber China."

38 Creemers, "Cyber China."

39 Creemers, "Cyber China."

40 Creemers, "Cyber China."

41 Lagerkvist, *After the Internet*.

42 Lagerkvist, *After the Internet*.

43 Shanshan Du, "Social Media and the Transformation of 'Chinese Nationalism': 'Igniting Positive Energy' in China since the 2012 London Olympics," *Anthropology Today* 30, no. 1 (2014): 5–8; Ki Deuk Hyun and Jinhee Kim, "The Role of New Media in Sustaining the Status Quo: Online Political Expression, Nationalism, and System Support in China," *Information, Communication & Society* 18, no. 7 (2015): 766–781; Ki Deuk Hyun, Jinhee Kim, and Shaojing Sun, "News Use, Nationalism, and Internet Use Motivations as Predictors of Anti-Japanese Political Actions in China," *Asian Journal of Communication* 24, no. 6 (2014): 589–604.

44 Sam Geall, ed., *China and the Environment: The Green Revolution* (Zed Books, 2013).

45 Jonathan Hassid, "Controlling the Chinese Media: An Uncertain Business," *University of California, Reprinted from Asian Survey* 48, no. 3 (2008): 414–430.

46 Baogang He and Mark E. Warren, "Authoritarian Deliberation: The Deliberative Turn in Chinese Political Development," *Perspectives on Politics* 9, no. 2 (2011): 269–289.

47 He and Warren, "Authoritarian Deliberation," 270.

48 He and Warren, "Authoritarian Deliberation," 281.

49 Min Jiang, "Authoritarian Deliberation on Chinese Internet," *Electronic Journal of Communication* 20 (2009); Katy E. Pearce and Sarah Kendzior, "Networked Authoritarianism and Social Media in Azerbaijan," *Journal of Communication* 62, no. 2 (2012):

283–298; Evgeny Morozov, *The Net Delusion: The Dark Side of Internet Freedom* (PublicAffairs, 2012); Nele Noesselt, "Microblogs and the Adaptation of the Chinese Party-State's Governance Strategy," *Governance* 27, no. 3 (2014): 449–468.

50 Interview: Song Jianing, Bureau Chief, CCTV Africa. Nairobi, Kenya, September 13, 2012.

51 Marsh, "Chinese State Television's 'Going Out' Strategy"; Zhang, "How Ready Is China for a China-Style World Order?"

52 Gagliardone, "China as a Persuader"; Gagliardone and Nyíri, "Freer but Not Free Enough?"

53 A fresh new set of studies have recently emerged on Russia's "whataboutism," indicating, for example, how the Russian government and its controlled media have mastered a strategy pointing at their critics' double standards to depotentiate their attacks and attach blame on those seeking to speak from a higher moral ground. See, for example, James Headley, "Challenging the EU's Claim to Moral Authority: Russian Talk of 'Double Standards,'" *Asia Europe Journal* 13, no. 3 (2015): 297–307.

54 George Lakoff, *The All New Don't Think of an Elephant! Know Your Values and Frame the Debate* (Chelsea Green Publishing, 2014).

55 Xi Jinping, "Remarks by H.E. Xi Jinping President of the People's Republic of China at the Opening Ceremony of the Second World Internet Conference."

56 Xinhua News Agency, "China Headlines: Xi Slams 'Double Standards,' Advocates Shared Future in Cyberspace," *Xinhua*, December 16, 2015, http://news. xinhuanet.com/english/indepth/2015-12/16/c_134924012.htm.

57 Li Yan, "Reforming Internet Governance and the Role of China," Focus Asia, Institute for Security and Development Policy, Stockholm 7 (2015), http://isdp.eu/content/uploads/ publications/2015-LiYan-Reforming-Internet-Governance-and-the-role-of-China.pdf.

58 As quoted in Lagerkvist, "Chinese Eyes on Africa," 127.

59 Interview: Daniel Berhane. Addis Ababa, May 10, 2013.

60 Xiaolan Fu, "Foreign Direct Investment, Absorptive Capacity and Regional Innovation Capabilities: Evidence from China," *Oxford Development Studies* 36, no. 1 (2008): 89–110; Xiaolan Fu, Carlo Pietrobelli, and Luc Soete, "The Role of Foreign Technology and Indigenous Innovation in the Emerging Economies: Technological Change and Catching-Up," *World Development* 39, no. 7 (2011): 1204–1212.

61 Ping Gao and Kalle Lyytinen, "Transformation of China's Telecommunications Sector: A Macro Perspective," *Telecommunications Policy* 24, no. 8 (2000): 719–730; Milton Mueller, *China in the Information Age: Telecommunications and the Dilemmas of Reform* (Greenwood

Publishing Group, 1997), 169; Bing Zhang, "Understanding China's Telecommunications Policymaking and Reforms: A Tale of Transition toward Liberalization," *Telematics and Informatics* 19, no. 4 (2002): 331–349.

62 China Unicom, the first company to enter into competition with former monopolist China Telecom, was created under a strategy defined as CCF (China-China-Foreign), by which a foreign partner of a venture invested in a joint venture, which, in turn, invested in China Unicom. As Zhang remarks, "this financing mechanism aimed to bypass the prohibition of foreign investments in telecommunications services and resolve the financing problem at the same time." After this practice was allowed for five years, it was later sanctioned as "irregular" by the newly created Ministry of Information and foreign investors had to draw back their investments. Zhang, "Understanding China's Telecommunications Policymaking and Reforms."

63 Interview: Representative of Huawei in Ethiopia. Addis Ababa, May 9, 2013.

64 Interview: Manager, Ethio Telecom. Addis Ababa, January 11, 2012.

65 Interview: ICT expert. Addis Ababa, December 30, 2011.

66 Interview: ICT expert. Addis Ababa, December 30, 2011.

67 Dalton, "Telecom Deal by China's ZTE, Huawei in Ethiopia Faces Criticism."

68 Iginio Gagliardone, "China and the African Internet: Perspectives from Kenya and Ethiopia/China y El Internet Africano: Perspectivas Desde Kenia y Etiopía," *Index. Comunicación* 3, no. 2 (2013): 67–82; Okuttah, "Safaricom Loosens China's Grip on Local Contracts with Sh14bn Tender; Margaret Wahito, "Kenya: China to Fund Kenya's Fibre Optic Project."

69 Binyavanga Wainaina, "How to Write about Africa," *Granta Magazine*, January 19, 2006, https://granta.com/how-to-write-about-africa/; Duncan Clarke, "Africa: How to Be an Expert," *The Guardian*, November 12, 2012, sec. World News, www.theguardian.com/world/2012/nov/12/africa-expert-celebrity-madonna.

70 Elizabeth C. Economy, "The Great Firewall of China: Xi Jinping's Internet Shutdown," *The Guardian*, June 29, 2018, sec. News, www.theguardian.com/news/2018/jun/29/the-great-firewall-of-china-xi-jinpings-internet-shutdown.

5 | IS IT REALLY ABOUT CHINA?

The securitization of development and its influence on Africa's information societies

This book was inspired by the need to understand whether and how China is influencing the shaping of information societies in Africa. The more I sought answers to these questions, and more specifically to whether China might be promoting a more authoritarian version of the Internet on the continent, the more I came across a different type of publicly embraced discourse, especially by heads of state and top-level bureaucrats, to justify some of the repressive measures that had become increasingly common across the continent, including Internet shutdowns and the boosting of surveillance. As a veteran computer scientist, who had observed the evolution of the information society in many African countries, put it: "In practice many countries copy China, but when they explain what they are doing they mention the West."[1]

Apart from very isolated cases,[2] when repressive measures have been adopted or proposed in countries as diverse as Uganda, Nigeria, Kenya, or Cameroon, it has not been China being held as an example for creating a supposedly more harmonious version of the information society. Across the continent, it has been the United States-backed anti-terrorism agenda, and the related securitization of development, which have offered much more easily exploitable arguments to justify and legitimize the repression of online communication and the persecution of Internet users.

In May 2016, before Yoweri Museveni was sworn in as Uganda's president for a fifth term, extending his rule to 35 years, Twitter, Facebook, and WhatsApp were blocked across the country. The justification offered by the director of Uganda's telecommunications regulator was that the censoring of social media was meant "to limit the possibility of terrorists taking advantage" of visits by dignitaries.[3] Statements such as this, in a harder or softer version, directly referring to terrorist threats or to a more generic need to guarantee national security, have proliferated since the beginning of the War on Terror and have increasingly become the norm. Even authorities in Ghana, a country with strong democratic credentials and relatively peaceful polity, have openly proclaimed their readiness to adopt repressive measures if needed. In an interview ahead of the 2016 general elections, representatives of Ghana's police force, when asked whether they would consider the possibility of shutting down the Internet or part of it, declared, "If people are churning out the type of information which is quite false then why not? The security of this nation is paramount."[4]

The exploitation of the ambivalences that have increasingly come to characterize the agendas of Western donors, seeking to concurrently promote human rights and ensure security at home and abroad, is not exclusive to the online sphere. It is part of a longer-term process of extraversion, which has allowed governments in Africa to make use of discourses and resources available at the international level to support domestic agendas and consolidate their power base. In the specific case of the Internet, however, the widespread tactics of exploiting the ambivalences of Western aid and foreign policy to justify surveillance and control is also indicative of the still hegemonic quality of discourses of the information society promoted in the West. It is only countries that had already severed their relationships with most Western donors, such as Zimbabwe under Robert Mugabe, which openly purported the strategy championed by China as an example.

The next two sections examine this process of extraversion and its contradictions. The first explores the rise of the securitization of development, before focusing on how it has influenced the strategies elaborated by governments in Ethiopia, Kenya, Ghana, and Rwanda to shape their national information spaces. It also reflects on the increasing uneasiness this agenda has produced for NGOs, making them vulnerable to attacks stressing their dependence on external ideas and resources. The second section examines instead how the hypocrisy that has come to characterize the United States' Internet agenda more specifically, as revealed by the leaks of the US National Security Agency contractor Edward Snowden, and other initiatives promoted in the field of Internet governance is increasingly threatening the idea and implementation of a free and open Internet.

The development–security nexus and the Internet

The attacks on the Twin Towers on September 11, 2001 have produced a rapid acceleration of the process of securitization of development, exacerbating ongoing trends and introducing new dynamics.

The increasing emphasis on the links between development and security has been located as the most recent component of the process of "neoliberal stabilization,"[5] which began with the structural adjustment policies of the 1980s and the drive towards democratization in the 1990s.[6] As Mark Duffield argued, connecting securitization with previous incarnations of development policy, "it is the deepening of the West's sovereign frontier through setting the moral standards and desired forms of comportment against which other actors must now measure, adjust and orchestrate themselves."[7] Ironically, as further illustrated below, this quest for normalization and stabilization of the relationship between Western donors and their recipients has led to numerous results going in the opposite direction. It has offered leverage to countries in the Global South – especially those under authoritarian rule – to fend off donors' demands in once critical areas such as human rights promotion or the support of local civil society, citing the need to focus on stability first.

The War on Terror has also led to the formulation of a new form of discourse, and a significant shift in priorities among most Western donors, "with terrorism occupying a central place and development concerns becoming subordinated to the security concerns of donor countries."[8] Before 2001, the Development Assistance Committee (DAC) had seldom placed security as a driver of development policy. After 9/11, this tendency was quickly reversed, stressing how "development co-operation does have an important role to play in helping to deprive terrorists of popular support and addressing the conditions that terrorist leaders feed on and exploit."[9] Since then, the development–security nexus has progressively become a trope for many development agencies. The United Kingdom's Department for International Development (DFID), once reluctant to intervene on security matters, has become accepting of arguments connecting development and security, incorporating them in its own policies, and intensifying collaborations with foreign policy and military institutions.[10] Japan's "trinity" of assistance, investment, and trade has been replaced by a "new trinity," characterized by assistance and a greater reliance on NGOs and the military, in a context of a scaled-up involvement in peacekeeping and military operations.[11]

While different donor agencies within the DAC maintained a certain degree of autonomy in setting their priorities,[12] their strategies have appeared to share at least two closely related features in the post-9/11 era of international development. First, the nexus between security and development, instead of being rooted in solid evidence and "lessons learned," has rather emerged as imposed from above, relying on the argument that there can't be development in conflict.[13] This position has been contested from different fronts, examining cases where development has indeed occurred in contexts of instability,[14] or indicating how "it would be impossible to attribute a reduction or increase in terrorist risk to a particular development intervention or set of policy initiatives."[15] This criticism, rather than leading to a more coherent theorization of the links between security and development, has largely been ignored, and the burden of realizing projects informed by the security–development framework spread across an increasingly variety of actors, from international institutions to private policy contractors.[16]

A second, more relevant feature for the arguments elaborated in this book is the articulation of a relationship between "our" security, as the security of Western countries from attacks originating from beyond their borders, and "their" security, in developing countries, with the former often taking priority over the latter.[17] This feature is important, as will become more apparent in the following sections, because of its contribution to further expose the hypocrisy of development agendas, seeking to promote values and strategies as supposedly beneficial for all, while representing in fact the interest of a minority. As articulated below, this contradiction has had profound consequences both in undermining the position of development actors, NGOs above all, who derived their legitimacy from their drive towards helping the marginalized or protecting their rights, rather than representing their funders, and in offering to governments in developing countries new opportunities to contest Western conditionality, framing it as one-sided and parochial, rather than having to justify themselves for their poor performance against widely shared standards.

Securitization and the weakening of the civil society

In recent years, the foreign aid industry has undergone an important shift. Whereas development workers until the late 1980s were mainly perceived – and often perceived themselves – as a rare species of internationalist idealists, the emergence of "failed and fragile states," such as Afghanistan and Somalia, and "new wars" in the Balkans and elsewhere contributed to the blurring of lines between the "neat" world of development and the "murky" field of national and international security. Although governments used development assistance throughout the Cold War to further their own interests in the context of superpower rivalry, aid workers generally agreed that these were regrettable circumstances. The end of the Cold War nurtured hopes that foreign aid would finally be free to focus solely on fighting poverty and inequality.[18]

This quote from Brown and Grävingholt's book *The Securitization of Foreign Aid* may depict a romantic view of the development worker, but does signal an important transition: from a perception of the "civil society" as a relatively unitary actor, whose involvement is considered beneficial for a more inclusive development process, to a more critical and contested view, rooted in the assimilation of the civil society into the gaze of security institutions.

The securitization of development has had profound consequences on how civil society organizations are perceived and can operate in developing countries. The polarizing language of the War on Terror has increasingly led to a separation – emanating from donor countries first – between "good" and "bad" elements of the civil society. As Howell and Lind have explained, the "good" civil society, as labeled in the Global North, is more accountable and "promotes or embodies liberal values such as democracy, rights, gender, racial and political equality."[19] On the contrary, the "bad" civil society is less transparent and formalized, and is potentially vulnerable to abuse by other organizations, including terrorists and organized crime. This distinction has been informed both by the drive towards combating the causes of terrorism and by the increasing demands placed on donor agencies for greater accountability and efficiency in times of austerity measures. It has – unsurprisingly – put pressure on groups representing Muslims, and it has led to increasing efforts to make populations at the margin more visible and legible.[20]

This distinction, however, has not remained an exclusive domain of donor countries. Governments in the Global South have increasingly made it theirs, in an apparent display of solidarity against terrorism, but also as a powerful tool to be turned against opponents. As illustrated below, especially when examining the case of Ethiopia, the separation between "good" and "bad," as arbitrary as it is, has been open to exploitation and has led to paradoxical outcomes. Groups that originated to promote values such as freedom of expression or respect for gender diversity – and that would thus register under the rubric of "good," according to the definitions adopted by donor agencies – have been labeled as "terrorist" and persecuted under newly instituted anti-terrorism laws. In combination with growing nationalistic tendencies, this critical gaze has been extended to cast a negative light on an increasingly broad variety of organizations. In Kenya, terms such as "evil society" have begun to enter political discourse.[21] NGOs, once largely praised for their contributions to promote supposedly universal values, have been increasingly accused of representing the interests of foreign powers, rather than contributing to locally rooted conceptions of development.

Securitization, extraversion, and state-building

The appropriation of the securitization agenda by – some – African governments can be located in a longer-term process of exploitation of the contradictions of foreign and aid policy for state- and nation-building in Africa. Analyzing this process offers another opportunity to understand African agency, in ways that highlight how some governments have been able to make use of their relation of dependency from foreign countries to their advantage, consolidating their grip on power and bolstering their own political projects. This is a form of agency that, while challenging Western hegemony, has tended to benefit the few, rather than the many, and has allowed political elites, often emerging from civil wars, to extend their control over their countries. By nominally accepting agendas promoted internationally, governments in Ethiopia, Rwanda, Uganda, or Chad have concurrently increased their leverage over Western donors, gaining room for enforcing centralized projects of development, while reducing the space for their opponents to contest them.

An increasing body of literature has emerged to explain this process. Jean-François Bayart has been among the first to expose the complexities and contradictions of the relationship between African states and the international system, seeking to chart an African history of extraversion.[22] As he explained, referring both to colonial and postcolonial periods:

> The leading actors in sub-Saharan societies [...] have turned the external environment into a major resource in the process of political centralization and economic accumulation, and also in the conduct of the social struggles of subaltern actors from the moment that they attempted to take control, even in symbolic ways, of the relations with the exterior on which those who dominate the society base their power.[23]

More specifically, using the wave of democratization that swept the continent in the 1990s as an example, he argued that:

The discourse of democracy is not more than yet another source of economic rents, comparable to earlier discourses such as the denunciation of communism or of imperialism in the time of the Cold War, but better adapted to the spirit of the age.[24]

This frame, while contested and not necessarily applicable to all countries on the continent, does fit increasingly common scenarios of the kind emerged in Ethiopia or Rwanda, where leaders have adopted the trappings of democracy, but have eviscerated them of their ability to function, as testified by electoral contests won by ruling parties or coalitions with majorities close to 100%.

More recently, comparative research has looked further into the connection between extraversion and securitization. For Jonathan Fisher and David Anderson, "the Ethiopian and Ugandan regimes have made extensive use of Western security initiatives since the 1990s to build militarized, strongly authoritarian states."[25] Governments have been:

> building trust within the donor relationship yet gaining increased control over securitization. This has involved each government explicitly permitting donors a major role in some areas of policy – socializing policy-making in social development and economic sectors in particular – while simultaneously pursuing the explicit "privatization" of other areas, especially defence and security policy.[26]

These tactics are a component of a broader – often paradoxical – process of illiberal state-building that has become increasingly common, especially among countries situated in conflict-ridden areas (e.g. the Horn of Africa). This process combines a "high modernist ideology, underpinning the belief that bureaucratic enclaves of excellence and huge infrastructure projects can qualitatively reconfigure domestic political-economic systems," with "a patriotic, 'broad tent' discourse [aimed to] bring a wide range of social groups in their [i.e. ruling elites'] fold, even when their material interests are manifestly contradictory: peasants and bankers; low-ranking bureaucrats and merchants."[27] It is paradoxical because it exploits – once again – elements of the liberal agenda of international development, such as the emphasis on state fragility, to consolidate illiberal, authoritarian, and centralized "grand plans" with little room for deviation.[28] It has turned the civil society from a counterweight to the state into a "collaborative partner in advancing the state's agenda: organizations which do not play this role are shut out, defunded, or dismantled,"[29] often resorting to discourses about dependency from external resources, both at the material and ideational level, as a justification for adopting repressive measures.

In this regard, Ethiopia represents a paradigmatic case of how these complex trends have been weaved together, allowing the country to continue registering as a "donor darling," while increasingly asserting an agenda that defies mainstream development policy. Even countries such as Kenya, however, with stronger democratic credentials, have made use of references to external and internal threats to stability, to justify increasingly repressive measures. The next sections chart the evolution of this process of extraversion – stressing the ability of national governments and political entrepreneurs to exploit contradictions in the international agenda to support domestic projects of state control – and its consequences on the shaping of national information societies.

Ethiopia – from tactics to strategy

In August 2009, the Ethiopian parliament enacted its first piece of legislation aimed specifically at combating terrorism. Framed as an attempt to comply with requests from the United Nations and the United States to take the fight against international terrorism to a global level, it created the legal preconditions to actually prosecute critical voices within Ethiopia (or Ethiopians in the diaspora). As indicated by the incarceration of journalists, bloggers, and political opponents that followed, a legal provision aligning with international demands was used not only to fight terrorists, but also to stifle dissent. Differently from other cases of extraversion, however, the Ethiopian government progressively turned this relation of dependency, the necessity to seize opportunities emerging internationally to advance its own goals, into a more stable and centrally owned strategy.

Ethiopia has been relatively late to enact a domestic anti-terrorism law, as compared to other countries that introduced similar legislations in the aftermath of 9/11 to comply with UN Security Council Resolution 1373, which requires states to ensure that "terrorist acts are established as serious criminal offences in domestic laws."[30] Coming into force only in mid-2009, Ethiopia's Anti-Terrorism Proclamation was framed nonetheless as a response to the Resolution passed eight years earlier and to international pressure to combat terrorism. This decision openly contradicted a report the Ethiopian government had filed in 2002 to the Counter-Terrorism Committee (CTC), the agency instituted to monitor state compliance with Resolution 1373. In its response to the CTC, the Ethiopian government did acknowledge its vulnerability to terrorist attacks from organizations such as Al-Qaeda and Somalia-based Islamic group Al-Ittihad Al-Islamia, but it also clearly indicated that existing legal instruments, including the 1957 Criminal Code and the 1974 Special Penal Code, were adequate both to counter terrorism and prosecute perpetrators of terrorist attacks.[31]

It should be noted that since 2006, Ethiopia has fought a war in Somalia, backed by the United States, in support of Somalia's Transitional Federal Government, a war that has led to the creation of Al-Shabaab, a terrorist group that – paradoxically – would become one of the most serious threats to peace in the Horn of Africa.[32] It has also witnessed a number of violent episodes, including an attack by the Ogaden National Liberation Front on a Chinese-run oilfield in 2007 that claimed the lives of 74 people, including nine Chinese.

However, when the Proclamation is considered not just in relation to the evolution of international and domestic terrorism, but also to other legal instruments the government of Ethiopia has been developing during the same period and to the type of individuals who have been targeted, it acquires a different, more pernicious meaning. The Anti-Terrorism Proclamation shares with the Charities and Societies Proclamation (2009), the Regulation for the Re-establishment of the Information Network Security Agency (INSA, 2011), and the Telecom Fraud Offences Proclamation (2012) the common goal of extending the government's "legitimate" sphere of action, while limiting the possibility for other actors – domestic and international – to influence policy and politics in Ethiopia. As a powerful example of how governments have been able to exploit the negative sentiment emerging against civil society organizations mentioned above and use it to increase control over them, the Charities and Societies Proclamation has restricted NGOs that receive more than 10% of their financing from foreign sources from engaging in human rights and advocacy activities. The Telecom Fraud Offences Proclamation has reaffirmed the state monopoly over telecommunications, imposing severe sanctions for any operator trying to compete with or bypass Ethio Telecom, and has extended the provisions of the Anti-Terrorism Proclamation to the online sphere (Article 6). Since its creation, the INSA, shaped in the guise of the US National Security Agency (NSA), has taken on the responsibility of "protecting" the national information space, "taking counter measures against information attacks," which the law frames as any "attack against the national interest, constitutional order, and nation's psychology by using cyber and electromagnetic technologies and systems."[33]

Examining the profiles of the individuals convicted under the Anti-Terrorism Proclamation helps to further clarify the motivations behind the law and to understand how, similar to what had been experienced in other countries, including Colombia, Nepal, the Philippines, and Uganda,[34] the Ethiopian government interpreted the global war against terrorism as an opportunity to pursue domestic enemies while fending off external pressure and condemnation. Out of the 33 individuals convicted under the Anti-Terrorism Proclamation between 2009 and 2014, 13 have been journalists.

Some of them have been accused of planning terrorist attacks on infrastructure, telecommunications, and power lines (Woubshet Taye and Reeyot Alemu); others of suporting Ginbot 7, an organization led by Berhanu Nega, who in the 2005 elections had won the seat of Mayor of Addis Ababa, and was included in the country's terror list soon after its establishment (Eskinder Nega, Abebe Gelaw, Fasil Yenealem, and Abebe Belew); two journalists working for the newspaper *Ye Musilmoch Guday* were charged with plotting acts of "terrorism, intending to advance a political, religious, or ideological cause," as part of a broader crackdown on Ethiopian Muslims (Solomon Kebede and Yusuf Getachew); and two Swedish journalists who had embedded themselves with the Ogaden National Liberation Front to cover the conflict in Southern Ethiopia were also charged under the Anti-Terrorism Proclamation, and pardoned by the president after having served 450 days in prison (Johan Persson and Martin Schibbye). Some of the journalists have been charged *in absentia*; those who were apprehended in Ethiopia were sentenced to up to 18 years in prison.

Numerous international organizations, including the Committee to Protect Journalists, Reporters Without Borders, Amnesty International, and Human Rights Watch have accused the Ethiopian government of taking advantage of a law they have labeled as "deeply flawed"[35] to persecute and silence critical voices. The government has responded to this criticism by reasserting the legitimacy of its acts.

Bereket Simon, one of Ethiopia's most influential political figures,[36] justified his government's decision to detain the two Swedish journalists by labeling international pressure to free the detainees as "a very wrong defence of foreign journalists who have been caught red-handed assisting terrorists."[37] Similarly, in 2014, Prime Minister Hailemariam Desalegn commented on the arrest of the Zone 9 bloggers, a group of individuals who took to the Internet to advocate for a greater respect of rights included in the Ethiopian Constitution itself by alleging their links with terrorist groups. As he remarked, "I don't think becoming a blogger makes somebody immune, if someone involves into this terrorist network that destabilizes my country."[38]

In an even more blatant display of the ability to exploit the anti-terrorism agenda to respond to external criticism, the late Prime Minister Meles Zenawi declared that Ethiopia had copied the Anti-Terror Proclamation "word for word" from laws adopted in the West. "We took from America, England and the European model of anti-terrorism laws," he said. "From these we have chosen the better ones ... the proclamation in every respect is flawless. It is better than the best anti-terrorism laws."[39] In an interview with BBC News, Meles' successor, Prime Minister Hailemariam Desalegn, offered a similar defense of the law, explaining that "if you compare the British terrorist law and that of ours, it's almost similar."[40]

On a pure textual level, Hailemariam was correct in saying that direct comparisons can be made to the laws of other countries. The clearest example comes from Article 6 of the Anti-Terror Proclamation.[41] As the article reads:

> Whosoever publishes or causes the publication of a statement
> that is likely to be understood by some or all of the members
> of the public to whom it is published as a direct or indirect
> encouragement or other inducement to them to the commission
> or preparation or instigation of an act of terrorism ...[42]

The United Kingdom's Terrorism Act of 2006 reads:

> This section applies to a statement that is likely to be
> understood by some or all of the members of the public to
> whom it is published as a direct or indirect encouragement or
> other inducement to them to the commission, preparation or
> instigation of acts of terrorism or Convention offences.[43]

The similarities in the text are obvious. The reliance on the Western-backed anti-terrorism agenda to pursue domestic goals, however, does not end with legal norms, but extends to the material and technological innovations that came with it. As revealed by the leaks of security contractor Edward Snowden, in the aftermath of 9/11, the US NSA:

> set up the Deployed Signals Intelligence Operations Center –
> also known as "Lion's Pride" – in Ethiopia's capital, Addis
> Ababa. [...] It began as a modest counterterrorism effort
> involving around 12 Ethiopians performing a single mission at
> 12 workstations. But by 2005, the operation had evolved into
> eight US military personnel and 103 Ethiopians, working at 46
> multifunctional workstations.[44]

In another leaked document, Katie Pierce, the officer in charge of Lion's Pride in 2005, explained, "The benefit of this relationship is that the Ethiopians provide the location and linguists and we provide the technology and training."[45]

Alongside Lion's Pride, the Ethiopian government's hunger for tools that could expand its ability to control communications led it to uniquely combine technologies purchased from the most diverse types of actors. ZTE, as the largest telecommunications provider in the country (as detailed in Chapter 3), offered a customer management database, which, in addition to collecting records of calls made in Ethiopia, could allow accessing content of text messages and audio of phone calls when needed. Another tool developed by ZTE, called ZXMT, relying on deep packet inspection to scan Internet traffic, is also likely to have been used in Ethiopia, even if unrefutable evidence is missing.

The Ethiopian authorities have also actively shopped in the European market for advanced surveillance technologies, acquiring tools to spy not only on individuals living in Ethiopia, but also on Ethiopians in the diaspora. FinSpy, a surveillance system sold by a firm first headquartered in the United Kingdom and later in Germany, was purchased by the Ethiopian government to allow the remote accessing of infected computers. Hacking Team, an Italian company providing "eavesdropping software" that "hides itself inside target devices" – which, ironically, was hacked in 2015, leading to 400 GB of private communications entering into the public domain – provided services to the Ethiopian government allowing it to acquire communications from opposition leaders and journalists in the diaspora.

As this complex web of legal and technical resources indicates, far from being pushed into complying with an agenda imposed from above, either by partners in the West or in the East, the Ethiopian government has displayed a remarkable ability to exploit the weaknesses of different agendas to strengthen its own political plan. As I sought to explain elsewhere,[46] this project itself contained significant flaws, especially related to the government's inability to allow a middle ground to emerge where at least some forms of criticism could be entertained, but is to date one of the clearest examples of the contradictions in which the securitization agenda has incurred in Africa.

Kenya – from resistance to reluctant compliance

Compared to Ethiopia, Kenya offers a contrasting – almost opposite – case of how the international securitization agenda intersected with domestic politics, one that illustrates nonetheless how the emphasis on measures focused on combating terrorism can have a chilling effect on online debates.

Similar to other countries in the Global South, in the aftermath of the attacks on the Twin Towers, Kenya was invested by pressures to swiftly introduce special legislation to fight national and international terrorism. The first response to such pressures came in 2003, when the Attorney General published the Suppression of Terrorism Bill (SOT), strongly supported by Western diplomats.[47] Kenya shared with Ethiopia a complex geostrategic position, because of its proximity to conflict-ridden areas, Somalia above all, and relative stability, making it a strong ally for Western countries, the United States in particular, in the fight against extremism in the region. In addition, the country had already suffered large-scale terrorist attacks, targeting both national and international interests: the 1980 bombing of the Norfolk Hotel and the 1998 attack on the American embassy in Nairobi.[48]

In stark contrast with Ethiopia, however, Kenya's vocal civil society was able to articulate a strong opposition to the antiterrorism bill. The resistance came from different corners of the Kenyan society. Kenyan media lamented the bill was elaborated without any public consultation.[49] Human rights groups stressed how numerous provisions would violate rights protected by the country's own Constitution. The most decisive opposition came from Kenyan Muslims in relation to a clause in the bill allowing arresting a person "who, in a public place wears an item of clothing ... in such a way ... as to arouse reasonable suspicion that he is a member or supporter of a declared terrorist organization."[50] As the Muslim community remarked, members might be targeted on the mere basis of their appearance as Muslim. Facing such broad opposition, the government eventually withdrew the bill. Also, a later attempt to pass similar legislation, based on a larger debate and incorporating concerns raised by civil society organizations, was opposed and ultimately dropped in 2006.[51]

Kenya thus seems to offer an example of how in a polity characterized by a greater balance of power among different political, social, and religious forces, stronger resistance could be articulated towards the imposition of a new norm from above, one that could have severe effects on the liberty of individuals and groups.

Kenya, at the same time, offers an example of how, in a context where securitization has become a recurrent feature in political debates, events can tilt the balance in favor of more repressive measures and greater control of communications. As introduced in Chapter 3, in 2007 and 2008, Kenyans witnessed one of the most tragic moments in the country's post-independence history, when the uncertain results emerging from national elections led to widespread violence across the country, with different ethnic communities turning against one another. The event ultimately led to the creation of a coalition government and the articulation of an increasingly insistent narrative about the need to bring peace back to the country. The same narrative also offered new space for introducing tighter controls on what individuals could or could not say. As Erik Hersman, one of Kenya's most influential technologists – behind the creation of systems such as Ushahidi that contributed to boost the country's image as an innovation hub – remarked:

> There is a battle between the people and the government. The government is monitoring SMS and other communications. The 2007–2008 post-election violence became the excuse for everything. Without that event there would be no foundations for any of the control that is now going on in the country. What is happening has not too much to do with censoring, but mostly with the big brother.[52]

The post-election crisis highlighted deep fault lines between groups within Kenya. The measures that followed were informed by a broader mandate to guarantee security and stability, rather than by a narrower focus on combating terrorism. The consequences of these initiatives, however, starkly resemble those that have come to characterize the application of the securitized development agenda highlighted above. The government was invested with greater powers to control citizens, developing relatively opaque relationships with private operators, which were asked to provide technical means to increase the ability to surveil and censor communications. The civil society, on the contrary, was weakened, especially in its ability to contest repressive measures and call for greater transparency. As a leading member of the coalition of civil society organizations emerging at the intersection between tech, governance, and human rights remarked:

> There is collusion between the security sector, the providers and other interest groups but this debate did not really take off, even in places such as Kiktanet [the country's leading mailing list where discussions about technology and society take place]. The problem is that there is not really civilian oversight over the monitoring and they claim it is an issue of national security. [...] We have a kind of smart repression: people have started to be afraid to speak on the phone under this administration.[53]

As highlighted by another Kenyan tech entrepreneur and activist, sidelining critical voices seeking to warn about measures aimed at combating terrorism, hate speech, and other forms of extreme dissent could lead to slowly sliding into a new form of authoritarianism, disempowering citizens more broadly: "The government is saying that they are monitoring SMS and they present peace as a justification. We are getting into a dictatorship, but people are euphoric about it. Society is brought into a kind of amnesia."[54]

In 2013 and 2015, Kenya witnessed two of the most tragic terrorist attacks in its recent history. The first was the siege of the Westgate shopping mall in Nairobi, where gunmen affiliated with the Somali extremist group Al-Shabaab killed 67 people and wounded another 175. The second was the shooting that took place at Garissa University, claiming the lives of 148 people, most of them students. The events shocked the country and also created a new opportunity to pass more stringent regulations aimed at fighting terrorism. On December 11, 2014, the Parliamentary Committee on National Security and Administration sent to parliament a new Security Laws Amendment Bill, containing several clauses restricting rights protected in the Kenyan Constitution, including freedom of speech and assembly. The security law made it easier to jail or fine journalists found guilty of undermining investigations or security operations through their broadcasts or publications.[55] Also in this case, civil society organizations held several campaigns to stop the bill, but this time the bill was eventually turned into law. Only eight clauses were later suspended by Kenya's High Court, on claims of unconstitutionality.

Further away from terrorism: how Ghana and Rwanda responded to the securitization agenda

Ethiopia and Kenya are examples of how the securitization agenda, while not necessarily determining a tightening of civic and political liberties, has offered new terrain for domestic politics to play out, often ending up strengthening incumbent leaders' grip on power. Ghana and Rwanda offer a relatively different perspective, one that further illustrates how different historical trajectories interact with international agendas.

In the case of Ghana, individual incidents, including in neighboring countries, have recently offered room to reconsider existing policies. As a journalist at the popular Citi FM in Accra remarked, referring to the deal struck by the United States and Ghana in 2016 to host two ex-Guantanamo detainees:

> At the time when the two Gitmo ex-detainees were being brought into the country there was a huge debate about us bringing them and having a replication of terrorists targeting us as a country. So at the time there were a lot of engagements among security agencies going round asking that we prepare ourselves for any intended terrorist attack. What also heightened the tension was the terrorist attack at the Grand Bassam resort in Ivory Coast. We were like, "Ivory Coast is just a neighboring country," so we told ourselves that we have to be prepared for any terrorist attacks.[56]

Ghana's long tradition of media freedom has so far prevented risks that these types of events could lead to measures actually impinging on people's liberties. Threats of Internet shutdowns have been generally interpreted by Ghanaian observers as attempts to gauge the temperature among citizens, rather than an imminent possibility the Internet would be blocked. As the Director of Ghana's Center for Democratic Development (CDD) explained:

> I think it was just a trial balloon. He [the Inspector General of Police] was just trying to throw up the idea and see what reaction he might get. But the pushback was swift. [...] Ghanaians will go far to protect the freedoms that they already have. I think citizens figured out, we don't really get a whole lot from the government, but this one – Internet freedom – you did not give it to us and we are not going to allow you to take it from us.[57]

Similar to Kenya, the system of checks and balances characterizing formal and informal institutions in Ghana has represented a powerful antidote towards excesses in national and international policymaking. As the trajectory of subsequent anti-terrorism bills in Kenya also indicates, however, relatively democratic and diverse polities remain vulnerable to change when events of larger scale occur, possibly producing a change in public opinion.

Compared to Ghana, Rwanda offers yet another variation of the direct and indirect consequences of the securitization of development and foreign policy. Rwandan authorities did not have to wait for 9/11 and the new wave of anti-terrorism policies that followed to create a complex apparatus of surveillance and control. The genocide in 1994 offered a strong enough rationale to enforce measures aimed at avoiding conflict and perpetrate individuals promoting hatred and divisiveness. Since the Rwandan Patriotic Front (RPF) took power after the genocide, a sophisticated system of formal and informal control was created to guarantee the presence of the state could be felt down to the lowest level of the Rwandan society and diversion and contestation could be easily identified and sanctioned. As Andrea Purdekova remarked, despite administrative reforms aimed at decentralizing the state, the government of Rwanda has created a system by which control is rather "dispatched" from the center to the peripheries.[58] Alongside the formal structures, other institutions have been created, including NGOs, to perform functions contributing to the achievement of goals defined by the center of power.

As Purdekova further specified, in some cases, the formal and informal institutions created by the Rwandan government to ensure control took direct inspiration from China, and from the work of Mao in particular. As she reported, through the words of one of her informants commenting on how in rural Rwanda a plethora of committees had been created to ensure individuals would check on one another: "The whole thing is copied from Mao Tse Tung. [...] In Tung's China, the idea was to have two thirds of people busy with different responsibilities."[59]

Taken together, the four cases account for a significant variation in the national responses to the global anti-terrorism agenda. They also highlight the fragility of the idea of a free and unfettered information space, which is increasingly under attack not just as the result of one type of influence or the rise of one specific actor, but as the combination of different forces, that need to be accounted for together, rather than in separation.

A free but securitized Internet?

The securitization of development and foreign policy has been characterized by the use of loaded language and the creation of sharp distinctions between "good" and "evil." As the previous sections indicated, this language and the policies underpinning it have offered new opportunities, especially for authoritarian regimes, to stifle dissent and reduce the space for even moderate forms of contestation to be articulated. In countries such as Ethiopia, this has had direct repercussions on the shaping of the national information society, introducing tools and arguments to identify and persecute online users.

Loaded and polarized language, however, has not been limited only to the urgency of combating terrorism. In the relatively more subdued arena of Internet governance, confrontations have also been stepped up, and all-encompassing narratives produced, framing some actors as protecting and others as threatening a supposed essence of the global Internet. Similar to the case of the anti-terrorism agenda, these narratives have prevented more nuanced analyses and explanations from being articulated and discussed. But they have also exposed some of the contradictions and biases of their promoters, including the United States, which have historically occupied a hegemonic position in shaping discourses on the global Internet.

As introduced in Chapter 4, the 2012 World Conference on International Telecommunications (WCIT) in Dubai, initially expected to be a relatively technical gathering to update the International Telecommunication Regulations (ITRs), became a highly political space for alternative ideas of the Internet to enter into direct competition with one another. The imagery of a new Cold War was evoked, and campaigns launched to name and shame the likes of the Chinese or Russian governments for trying to impose their ideas of a fragmented information space and warn them to take their "hands off the Internet." Some commentators compared the WCIT with Yalta, the conference held at the end of the Second World War to negotiate new spheres of influence for the winning powers. As they argued, evoking the specter of a new Cold War over the Internet, "after Dubai, only a binary world seemed to be left – most of the developing world (minus India) had sided with the cybersovereignty advocates. WCIT had morphed into a battle that, effectively, resulted in the West against the rest."[60]

The heightened tones used to describe the events in Dubai both reveal and conceal key features that have come to characterize a more contested phase of Internet governance, where different actors are seeking to advance competing ideas of the Internet: the creation of opposing camps led by national governments, accompanied by the weakening of the role of the civil society as an independent actor in shaping decisions on the Internet, and the – apparently contradictory – emergence of new spaces for governments and companies to cooperate to enhance their ability to gather information on the activities of Internet users.

A weak global civil society and a fading idea of the Internet

The "Hands off the Internet" campaign, launched just before the WCIT, was successful in creating the impression of two neatly separated camps battling in Dubai, one to keep the Internet free from government interference, the other to impose greater control over online communications. As Jermyn Brook, the Chair of the Global Network Initiative, wrote in *The New York Times*:

> A chorus of human rights groups, diplomats, companies and technologists has achieved something remarkable. They are shining a media spotlight on the most boring international conference you have never heard of: an obscure gathering of governments called the World Conference on International Telecommunications, or W.C.I.T. Campaigners and companies alike are concerned by the prospect of authoritarian states using the opaque processes of diplomacy to grab greater control over the Internet.[61]

By developing a simplified narrative, stressing distinctions between "free" and "unfree," "open" and "closed," along the lines of other initiatives aimed at bringing relatively localized conflicts or niche disputes to global attention, the campaign sought to create a higher moral ground from which to sanction those who contested or evaded the norm. Only a few scholars and experts, who had been following Internet governance debates since their inception, identified and highlighted the contradictions and the risks of this strategy. As Michael Gurstein noted, with a touch of irony:

> No one in their right minds wants anti-democratic Russia, or Great Firewall China, or 13th century Saudi Arabia dictating what goes over the Internet or as the term goes, "governing the Internet." But equally, no responsible party with any knowledge of the Internet really believes in the catch phrase "Hands off the Internet" – there are too many hands/agencies/even national and global organizations currently with their "Hands on the Internet."[62]

As Gurstein continued, through the spin created by the "Hands off the Internet" coalition, corporate actors that strongly backed the campaign were, at the same time, able to hide some of their interests in maintaining the status quo in Internet regulation. As he added:

Google as with most of the major US-based global Internet firms have something of an Internet related tax problem. Being global in a cyberworld without boundaries they are able to move their revenues and costing around the world more or less at will to find those countries which have the most beneficial tax regimes.[63]

Other scholars of Internet governance, including Milton Mueller, appeared to share this vision, and further explained how the simplified narrative promoted in Dubai hid arguably legitimate requests from governments in the Global South to encourage Internet companies such as Google, SourceForge, or GoDaddy to provide basic services in their countries.[64]

The strongest criticism, however, was directed at the civil society, which in previous critical moments in the Internet governance debate (e.g. World Summit on the Information Society) had been able to articulate a relatively independent vision of the future of the global Internet, while in Dubai found itself flattened on the position of hegemonic powers and large corporate agents. In a separate piece, Gurstein sought to chart a more visionary role that the civil society could have played, if it wanted to keep true to its previous commitments:

It would seem that the most appropriate position for CS [civil society] in the emerging "Cold War" is one of "non-alignment" where CS recognizes the validity of certain elements in the stance of both camps including support for free expression and open access on the one hand, and of digital inclusion and a fair distribution of the economic benefits of the Internet on the other; and on the other hand rejects other elements of these camps–attempts to restrict free expression on one side and an absolutist anti-statist anti-regulatory position regarding the governance of the Internet on the other.

But particularly the CS position would be characterized by its commitment to the governance of the Internet as a global public good and to the operation of the Internet in the global public interest. In this way CS would reject support for an Internet dominated by private corporate interests as well as one supporting the interests of control oriented governments who would use the Internet for repression and as a way to enhance internal control.[65]

The ideal of a civil society united in defense of the Internet as a public good, and articulating positions that are alternative to both state and corporate agents, is not just a memory from the past. Just a few months before Dubai, a coalition of civil society organizations had successfully come together exactly in defense of that ideal, when seeking to halt legislation discussed in the American Congress and aimed at giving companies and public authorities new tools to pursue copyright violations. The proposed bills, known as the "Stop Online Piracy Act (SOPA)" and the "PROTECT IP Act" (PIPA), were opposed mostly because of the excessive powers they could have given to big players – the US government and entertainment companies – to persecute smaller ones, including those based on user-generated content. As Yochai Benkler and his colleagues illustrated, through the analysis of the mobilization that ultimately led Congress to drop the bills, this was a powerful example of how "the networked public sphere enabled a dynamic and diverse discourse that involved both individual and organizational participants and offered substantive discussion of complex issues contributing to affirmative political action."[66]

In this case, the civil society was indeed able to articulate a nuanced and independent position, able both to give voice to peripheral nodes of the campaign, which were seeking to bring clarity on relatively complex issues, and to mobilize support across the political spectrum.[67] In Dubai, this spirit seemed drowned by the insistence on the need to combat a common enemy, whose features were magnified to an extent that prevented the most reflective voices from recognizing some of the claims made by representatives of different camps.

Big players and deep packet inspection

Alongside the debacle of the civil society as an independent actor, able to chart an alternative and more inclusive vision of the information society, something even more troubling, but little reported, for the future of the global Internet took place in Dubai. Just days before the main conference, where accusations were traded between opposing factions, offering the impression of irreconcilable positions being articulated on the Internet and its regulation, another ITU-led gathering took place. Known as the World Telecommunication Standardization Assembly (WTSA), the meeting was part of a series of events held every four years by the standards-setting body of the ITU (the ITU-T) to update and consolidate its work.

In stark contrast with the polarized tones of the WCIT, representatives at the WTSA were swift in passing a new standard on the "Requirements for Deep Packet Inspection in Next Generation Networks," or "Y.2770." Discussions happened behind closed doors and no drafts were circulated before a final decision was made – attracting criticism on the "lack of transparency of the ITU-T in contrast to other leading global standards organizations."[68] A slip-up of the ITU-T secretariat, however, allowed Australian CryptoParty activist Asher Wolf to get hold of some of the preparatory documents.[69] Neither in the files that had become available before the meeting nor in the official communications of the ITU-T were there signs of a fracture between the "free" and the "un-free" world, between those who wanted more control and those advocating for an open Internet. The standardization of deep packet inspection (DPI) seemed to have found support both in the East and the West, among governments and corporate agents.

As numerous scholars and activists have pointed out, however, the standardization and normalization of DPI poses a fundamental threat to the very essence of the Internet, leading some to ask whether it may represent "the end of the Net as we know it."[70]

As Milton Mueller explained, "DPI introduces 'intelligence' into what has often been called a 'dumb' network, facilitating comprehensive surveillance and discrimination of data packets moving through the network."[71] The protocols on which the Internet is based were originally designed in such a way that only the source and destination addresses of a packet of information need to be read in order for that information to be delivered correctly. There is no need to have access to the "payload" – the content of the packet – that contains the text, images, files, or applications transmitted by the user. Lawrence Lessig described this feature of Internet architecture with the metaphor of a "day-dreaming postal worker" and stressed how this minimalism in design "reflected both a political decision about disabling control and a technological decision about optimal network design."[72]

DPI represents a fundamental threat to the principles that inspired this design. It offers to powerful actors – corporate or government agents with access to Internet infrastructure – the possibility of instantly reading all content that transits through the network and acting based on a set of rules that are often defined opaquely and beyond public scrutiny. As Milton Mueller continued, building on Lessig's metaphor:

> Now imagine a postal worker who is not daydreaming, but instead: Opens up all packets and letters; Reads the content; Checks it against databases of illegal material and when finding a match sends a copy to the police authorities; Destroys letters with prohibited or immoral content; Sends packages for its own mail-order services to a very fast delivery truck, while the ones from competitors go to a slow, cheap sub-contractor.[73]

DPI, while disrupting the original architecture on which the Internet was based, fulfills both the interests of corporations interested in managing networks more efficiently, promising the creation of "fast lanes" for those who can afford to pay for them, and of governments – especially in authoritarian regimes – enabling them to control – and possibly suppress – unwanted content in real time.

Against this background, the events in Dubai acquire new meanings. The perception produced by campaigns such as "Hands off the Internet" was of opposed coalitions seeking to promote radically different ideas of the Internet. The reality emerging from the consensus around DPI depicted a bleaker picture, where powerful actors – state and corporate, from the East and the West – were able to come together in defense of their different, but compatible and complementary, interests, enforcing technical measures that profoundly threatened users' ability to remain in control of their data and online experience.

This is just another example of how an excessive focus on China – and other countries that align to its positions – as a potential disruptor of the balance of power in the global information society, risks to conceal other, deeper, and potentially more troubling forces. Shouting "Hands off the Internet" may succeed in maintaining and possibly reinforcing a higher moral ground for those actors that have historically dominated debates on the global Internet, but may delay a much-needed reality check on what other actors and processes are eroding the idea of a free and open Internet.

Conclusion

Grand narratives, almost by definition, are deceiving, as they seek to bundle together heterogeneous elements, and to offer apparently simple interpretations of a complex reality. As this chapter has illustrated, they can also be exploited to pursue goals that are significantly different from those that first informed their emergence.

Trends and visions emerging from the West and from the East have tended to be framed as opposite, but they can be recombined in new hybrids on the ground, and in some areas, such as increased control over what users do, they actually tend to overlap in silent but pervasive ways.

Notes

1 Interview: Computer scientist. Johannesburg, South Africa, January 22, 2018.

2 Kabweza, "Chinese Style Internet Censorship Coming to Zimbabwe – President Mugabe." Zimbabwe's former president Robert Mugabe, was the only head of state to openly declare the need to adopt measures of the kind developed in China to control and shape the Internet in Africa.

3 Reuters, "Uganda Blocks Social Media, Clamps down before President Sworn In," *Reuters*, May 12, 2016, https://af.reuters.com/article/africaTech/idAFKCN0Y30YC

4 GhanaWeb, "Shutdown Social Media if Necessary – Group," *GhanaWeb*, 2016, www.ghanaweb.com/GhanaHomePage/NewsArchive/Shutdown-social-media-if-necessary-Group-443682.

5 Mark Duffield, *Development, Security and Unending War: Governing the World of Peoples* (Polity, 2007).

6 Nancy Thede, "Policy Coherence for Development

and Securitisation: Competing Paradigms or Stabilising North–South Hierarchies?" *Third World Quarterly* 34, no. 5 (2013): 784–799.

7 Duffield in Thede, "Policy Coherence for Development and Securitisation."

8 Thede, "Policy Coherence for Development and Securitisation," 794.

9 DAC, "A Development Co-Operation Lens on Terrorism Prevention: Key Entry Points for Action," DAC High Level Meeting, 2003.

10 Eamonn McConnon, "Fighting Poverty to Fight Terrorism: Security in DFID's Development Policy during the War on Terror," *Forum for Development Studies* 41 (2014): 135–157.

11 Koshida Kiyokazu, "Militarization of Japan ODA," *Reality of Aid*, 2004, www.realityofaid.org/wp-content/uploads/2013/02/2004Oct_security-agenda-and-development.pdf.

12 Brown and Grävingholt, *The Securitization of Foreign Aid*.

13 David Chandler, "The Security–Development Nexus and the Rise of 'Anti-Foreign Policy,'" *Journal of International Relations and Development* 10, no. 4 (2007): 362–386.

14 Cramer in Jude Howell and Jeremy Lind, *Counter-Terrorism, Aid and Civil Society: Before and after the War on Terror* (Palgrave Macmillan, 2009).

15 Jo Beall, Thomas Goodfellow, and James Putzel,

"Introductory Article: On the Discourse of Terrorism, Security and Development," *Journal of International Development: The Journal of the Development Studies Association* 18, no. 1 (2006): 51–67

16 Chandler, "The Security–Development Nexus and the Rise of 'Anti-Foreign Policy.'"

17 McConnon, "Fighting Poverty to Fight Terrorism"; Beall et al., "Introductory Article."

18 Stephen Brown and Jörn Grävingholt, *The Securitization of Foreign Aid* (Springer, 2016), 7.

19 Howell and Lind, *Counter-Terrorism, Aid and Civil Society*, 48.

20 Howell and Lind, *Counter-Terrorism, Aid and Civil Society*.

21 Jennifer Brass, "Kenya's Clampdown on Civil Society Is against Its Self-Interest," *The Conversation*, 2016, http://theconversation.com/kenyas-clampdown-on-civil-society-is-against-its-self-interest-62019.

22 Jean-François Bayart, "Africa in the World: A History of Extraversion," *African Affairs* 99, no. 395 (2000): 217–267.

23 Bayart, "Africa in the World," 219.

24 Bayart, "Africa in the World," 226.

25 Jonathan Fisher and David M. Anderson, "Authoritarianism and the Securitization of Development in Africa," *International Affairs* 91, no. 1 (2015): 137.

26 Fisher and Anderson, "Authoritarianism and the Securitization of Development in Africa," 143.

27 Will Jones, Ricardo Soares de Oliveira, and Harry Verhoeven,

Africa's Illiberal State-Builders (Refugee Studies Centre, 2012), 6.

28 Mutebi in Jones et al., *Africa's Illiberal State-Builders*, 8.

29 Jones et al., *Africa's Illiberal State-Builders*, 8

30 UN Security Council, "Resolution 1373" (2001), 2.

31 Wondwossen Demissie Kassa, "Examining Some of the Raisons D'Etre for the Ethiopian Anti-Terrorism Law," *Mizan Law Review* 7, no. 1 (2014), www.ajol.info/index.php/mlr/article/view/100534.

32 Ken Menkhaus, "The Crisis in Somalia: Tragedy in Five Acts," *African Affairs* 106, no. 424 (2007): 357–390; Ken Menkhaus, *Somalia: State Collapse and the Threat of Terrorism* (Routledge, 2013), 364.

33 Government of Ethiopia, "Information Network Security Agency Re-Establishment Proclamation No. 808/2013," 2013.

34 International Commission of Jurists, "Assessing Damage, Urging Action: Report of the Eminent Jurists Panel on Terrorism, Counter-Terrorism and Human Rights" (Geneva, 2009).

35 Human Rights Watch, "Ethiopia: Terrorism Law Decimates Media," *Human Rights Watch*, May 3, 2013, www.hrw.org/news/2013/05/03/ethiopia-terrorism-law-decimates-media.

36 Bereket Simon has served different institutional roles since the EPRDF came to power, including Minister of Communications and Special Advisor to the Prime Minister.

37 Voice of America, "Ethiopian PM Defends Anti-Terror Law, Condemns Critics," *VOA*, 2012, www.voanews.com/a/ethiopian-pm-defends-anti-terror-law-condemns-critics-138976759/159572.html.

38 Jacey Fortin, "Ethiopia: Bloggers and Journalists Are Charged as Terrorists," *The New York Times*, July 18, 2014, www.nytimes.com/2014/07/19/world/africa/ethiopia-bloggers-and-journalists-are-charged-as-terrorists.html.

39 Blain Biset, "Ethiopia's Anti-Terrorism Law Squelches Opposition, Activists Say," *Inter Press Service*, 2012, www.ipsnews.net/2012/12/ethiopias-anti-terrorism-law-squelches-opposition-activists-say/.

40 BBC, "Ethiopia Defends Dissident Arrest," *BBC News*, July 11, 2014, sec. Africa, www.bbc.com/news/world-africa-28272112.

41 Patrick Griffith, "Ethiopia's Anti-Terrorism Proclamation and the Right to Freedom of Expression," *Freedom Now*, 2013, www.freedom-now.org/news/ethiopias-anti-terrorism-proclamation-and-the-right-to-freedom-of-expression/.

42 Government of Ethiopia, "Proclamation No. 652/2009 of 2009, Anti-Terrorism Proclamation (2009)," www.refworld.org/docid/4ba799d32.html.

43 Government of the United Kingdom, Terrorism Act 2006 (2006), www.legislation.gov.uk/ukpga/2006/11/section/1.

44 Nick Turse, "How the NSA Built a Secret Surveillance Network for Ethiopia," *The Intercept,* September 13, 2017, https://theintercept.com/2017/09/13/nsa-ethiopia-surveillance-human-rights/.

45 Turse, "How the NSA Built a Secret Surveillance Network for Ethiopia."

46 Gagliardone, *The Politics of Technology in Africa.*

47 Howell and Lind, *Counter-Terrorism, Aid and Civil Society,* 139.

48 Bachmann, Jan, "Kenya and International Security: Enabling Globalisation, Stabilising 'Stateness', and Deploying Enforcement," *Globalizations* 9, no. 1 (2012): 125–143.

49 Bachmann, "Kenya and International Security."

50 *Kenya Gazette* as quoted in Bachmann, "Kenya and International Security."

51 This did not mean, however, that the government remained idle. While the legislative route was blocked by the Kenyan civil society, the government was able to make use of the financial and technical support coming from the United States to develop or strengthen counter-terrorism structures. In 2003, a Joint Terrorism Task Force was created, followed the next year by a National Security Advisory Committee and a National Counter Terrorism Centre.

52 Interview: Erik Hersman, entrepreneur. Nairobi, Kenya, April 29, 2013.

53 Interview: Mugambi Kiai, Open Society Foundation. Nairobi, Kenya, April 24, 2013.

54 Interview: Phares Kariuki, entrepreneur. Nairobi, Kenya, April 29, 2013.

55 As the law read, "any person who, without authorization from the National Police Service, broadcasts any information which undermines investigations or security operations relating to terrorism commits an offence and is liable of conviction to a term of imprisonment for a term not exceeding three years or to a fine not exceeding five million shillings, or both."

56 Interview: Obrempong Yaw Ampofo, Journalist. Accra, Ghana, February 23, 2018.

57 Interview: Kwesi Prempeh, Executive Director, Journalist, Centre for Democratic Development. Accra, Ghana, February 24, 2018.

58 Andrea Purdeková, "'Even if I Am Not Here, There Are so Many Eyes': Surveillance and State Reach in Rwanda," *The Journal of Modern African Studies* 49, no. 3 (2011): 475–497.

59 Purdeková, "'Even if I Am Not Here, There Are so Many Eyes,'" 493.

60 Klimburg, "The Internet Yalta," 3.

61 Jermyn Brooks, "Opinion: Hands off the Internet!" *The New York Times*, December 6, 2012, sec. Opinion, www.nytimes.com/2012/12/07/opinion/hands-off-the-internet.html.

62 Michael Gurstein, "(Whose) Hands off (What) Internet? Some Reflections on WCIT 2012," *Gurstein's Community Informatics*, 2012, http://gurstein. wordpress.com/2012/12/09/ whose-hand-off-what- internet-some-reflections- on-wcit-2012/.

63 Gurstein, "(Whose) Hands off (What) Internet?"

64 Milton Mueller, "What Really Happened in Dubai?" *Internet Governance Project*, December 13, 2012, www.internetgovernance. org/2012/12/13/what-really- happened-in-dubai/.

65 Michael Gurstein, "Civil Society and the Emerging Internet Cold War: Non-Alignment and the Public Interest," *Gurstein's Community Informatics*, February 11, 2013, https://gurstein. wordpress.com/2013/02/11/ civil-society-and-the-emerging- internet-cold-war-non-alignment- and-the-public-interest/.

66 Yochai Benkler et al., "Social Mobilization and the Networked Public Sphere: Mapping the SOPA-PIPA Debate," *Political Communication* 32, no. 4 (2015): 595.

67 Benkler et al., "Social Mobilization and the Networked Public Sphere."

68 Emma Llanso and Alissa Cooper, "Adoption of Traffic Sniffing Standard Fans WCIT Flames," *Center for Democracy & Technology*, 2012, https://cdt.org/blog/ adoption-of-traffic-sniffing-standard- fans-wcit-flames/.

69 "WCIT: National Governments' Control over the Internet May Be a Side-Effect," *Infosecurity Magazine*, December 6, 2012, www.infosecurity-magazine. com:443/news/wcit-national- governments-control-over-the/.

70 Bendrath and Mueller, "The End of the Net as We Know It?"

71 Bendrath and Mueller, "The End of the Net as We Know It?" 1143.

72 Lawrence Lessig, *Code: And Other Laws of Cyberspace* (ReadHowYouWant, 2009), 32.

73 Bendrath and Mueller, "The End of the Net as We Know It?" 1148.

6 | THE FUTURE OF THE GLOBAL INTERNET

This book began with a reminder of the once widely shared expectations the Internet would represent a – possibly fatal – threat for the Communist Party of China (CPC). Since those predictions were formulated almost two decades ago, the CPC not only has not succumbed to online mobilizations and coordination; it has demonstrated a remarkable ability to contain – and persecute – dissent while incorporating innovation in ICTs into the country's development trajectory. It has proved so good at it that Western expectations the Internet would have changed China have later turned into fears that authoritarian China could transform the global Internet, exporting its model abroad. The 2016 US elections have added an even more dramatic twist to this story.

Two years after the election of Donald Trump, a group of popular American scholars came together to ask not whether the Internet could (still) democratize China, but whether authoritarianism might have actually taken hold in the United States, also through the support of the Internet.[1] Reflecting on the history of Russian efforts to interfere with US elections, they compared unsuccessful attempts during the Cold War, tamed – they argued – by the role of mediated platforms and professional gatekeepers, with the arguably more incisive tactics deployed in 2016, when the effects of traditional news gatekeeping had weakened and distinguishing between truth and falsehood had become more complex.[2] One of the tropes of Internet libertarianism – that non-institutional forms of communication are freer from power and more able to report information that mainstream media are perceived as unable or unwilling to reveal – had been turned on its head. A foreign power had exploited people's credulity, their belief in the independence of content shared across social media, to gain political advantage and support the ascent to power of a leader with authoritarian tendencies.

***

In his 2013 novel *The Circle*, Dave Eggers narrated the story of a powerful Internet company moved by the belief that using innovation to make individuals more transparent was the key to building a better society, where individuals would strive to be their best and act – under the gaze of their peers – in the interest of the broader community. As Eggers described:

> To use any of the Circle's tools, and they were the best tools, the most dominant and ubiquitous and free, you had to do so as yourself, as your actual self, as your TruYou. The era of false identities, identity theft, multiple user names, complicated passwords and payment systems was over. Anytime you wanted to see anything, use anything, comment on anything or buy anything, it was one button, one account, everything tied together. [...] TruYou changed the Internet, in toto, within a year. Though some sites were resistant at first, and free-internet advocates shouted about the right to be anonymous online, the TruYou wave was tidal and crushed all meaningful opposition. Overnight, all comment boards became civil, all posters held accountable. The trolls, who had more or less overtaken the internet, were driven back into darkness.[3]

Playing with tropes derived from both utopian and dystopian narrations, mixing beliefs in the power of technology to create a perfect society with fears of instituting systems from which people cannot escape, Eggers sought to describe a non-distant future emanating from the American West Coast. The imposition of a real-name policy and the progressive institutionalization of a *social credit* system, which maps people's routine behaviors to determine and publicly share their trustworthiness score,[4] however, make his narration possibly a better fit to describe present-day China.

***

These two apparently opposite stories account for the power of technology to promote new forms of imagination, but also highlight the risks of embracing for too long the foundational myths sparked when an innovation emerges and failing to recognize how technology can progressively transform, often in dramatic ways. Cognizant of this risk, I sought to bring new evidence to the debate on the present and future of the Internet, examining both a physical and imaginative space where competing technologies, actors, and discourses meet, clash, and possibly generate new hybrids. I strived to let facts guide interpretations of emerging patterns, even when these apparently contradict expectations about how a specific actor would behave. This chapter concludes by returning to some of these key patterns, also suggesting some alternative interpretations and opportunities for future research and action.

China–Africa and the Internet: what we know so far

This book has sought to cut through simplistic narratives depicting China as either a neocolonial power seeking to impose its model abroad or a benevolent partner acting to take South–South cooperation in new directions. Building on the comparative analysis of the evolution of national information societies in Ethiopia, Rwanda, Ghana, and Kenya, as well as on a broader continental examination of Chinese support to the development of ICTs, it has offered material to answer questions that have become increasingly pressing since China stepped up its involvement in media and telecommunications overseas.

A number of empirically grounded arguments have been made throughout the book and can be summarized here, to respond in particular to claims that have been made about China's negative influence on the African Internet.

First, China does not appear to have actively promoted its model abroad. Unlike other donor countries that have openly sought to affirm the values and strategies that have guided the evolution of their own media – including new media – when providing international assistance, the Chinese government has remained relatively silent about the advantages of the model it developed to shape its domestic media and new media system when exported abroad.

Second, despite claims of a new Cold War over the Internet, dividing the world into two camps, China has not displayed an authoritarian bias when providing assistance, displaying greater friendliness towards countries that are similar to itself. China has offered support to countries that have shown a strong commitment towards an open Internet, allowing a plurality of actors to contribute, at different points in time and with varying degrees, to the shaping of their national information societies. It has similarly helped countries that have displayed greater similarities with, and interest in, the system China has itself developed. Ethiopia is the clearest example. But it is the lack of substantive funding to the development of the Internet in Rwanda, the country that arguably presents the most marked affinities with a system of the kind that emerged in China – for the level of sophistication of its apparatus of control and ability to rally private actors and civil society organizations around a vision of innovation emanating from the center of power – that offers a particularly strong backing to this argument.

Third, Chinese support to the development of ICTs, in democratic and authoritarian regimes, does not appear to have led to an increase of authoritarian tendencies. This argument is relatively less straightforward than the previous two, mostly because of the variety of factors that may contribute to the closing or opening of the information space at the national level. As explained throughout the book and further discussed below, the securitization of development promoted by the United States has offered strong arguments to justify measures that seem to be taking African countries closer to the more controlled and contained idea of the Internet that emerged in China. Going in the opposite direction, the rise to power of Abiy Ahmed, appointed as Ethiopia's Prime Minister in 2018, also in response to popular protests and demands, has created a path towards a potential opening of the country's information space, marked by the release of political prisoners, including journalists and bloggers, and the intention of liberalizing telecommunications. It will be interesting to map whether this change will also lead Chinese actors involved in the Ethiopian ICT sector to change the course of their activities, adapting to new demands and taking on the new reform agenda. Ethiopia could thus become an example of how a country that was heavily supported by China in its stubborn project to maintain a monopoly over ICTs can transition towards creating a relatively more open information space, possibly still with China as its ally.

China–Africa and the Internet: a more speculative account

The answers provided above seem to offer a relatively reassuring picture of the role China has had when providing assistance in the ICT sector in Africa. Some of the processes examined throughout the book, however, are also open to other, less benign interpretations, especially when the focus is shifted towards longer-term consequences and greater attention is paid to the specific forms of technopolitics emerging from the interaction between technologies, discourses, and actors from China and from Africa. Some of the arguments I make below are more speculative and in need of further research to be adequately supported. They are important, nonetheless, even in the form of hypotheses, to appreciate new, emerging processes that can significantly influence the future of the global Internet.

One question that lingered throughout the book, but to which it was not possible to offer a definite answer, is whether China has strategically played to some of the weaknesses and contradictions of its adversaries in order to promote its own agenda. It is well known how, in the long history of China, apart from a few exceptions, its leaders have sought to avoid direct confrontations with their adversaries and preferred strategies that could slowly consume their enemies or force them to eventually recognize defeat.[5] Has any element of this strategy informed Chinese actions in the development of the Internet at a national and international level? Chapter 5 illustrated how numerous leaders in Africa have played to the contradictions of the anti-terrorism agenda to consolidate power and fend off criticism emerging from Western donors and the international community. China itself has used a similar strategy, displaying solidarity towards the global fight against violent extremism, while strengthening and legitimizing new forms of control.

Is it possible that Chinese leaders, when they decided to venture into the ICT sector in Africa, realized how it was not necessary to openly articulate a discourse emphasizing control and security, because this discourse was already available and was actually being promoted by its adversaries? Answering this question may offer new elements to the argument that in the end, the Chinese government may indeed have an interest in the promotion of a more authoritarian and securitized version of the Internet, especially since a proliferation of this kind of model may lead to perceive its own strategies as less eccentric. Reflecting on this issue through the lenses of technopolitics – and thus emphasizing the interconnectedness and mutual influences between networks of technologies, actors, and discourses – it can be argued that for China, it was enough to offer material support for technological development to a specific type of actor – the state – for a discourse emphasizing control and security to emerge.

The inaccessibility of the highest levels of decision-making in China makes it particularly complicated to offer clear answers to these questions. But it can be further argued that this type of reasoning also resonates with some of the basic principles informing Marxist analysis on base and superstructure. This model has been criticized from many fronts, emphasizing the co-constitutive relationship between material and ideational forms of production, and many arguments have been advanced on how Chinese politicians have progressively abandoned Marx as a guide, especially when it comes to creating a new society led by the proletariat. Marxist thinking, however, is still informing numerous aspects of how the Chinese intelligentsia analyzes the forces shaping our world.[6] The support to information societies in Africa would be another example of this use of Marxism as an analytical tool on which to build empirically informed strategies. This would explain how the support of the technological base – providing resources to strengthen the position of the state and the technological solutions championed by it – could eventually lead to changes in the superstructure, on ideas of the Internet and its function in society. Again, these arguments are more tentative than other made in this book, and need further investigation and collaborative research, but offer an attractive vantage point through which to explore competing strategies for the shaping of ideas on the information society.

Old hypocrisy and new paths for the liberation of the Internet

While China has tended to act subtly, the United States under the presidency of Donald Trump has become increasingly loud, challenging some of the very principles of liberalism that have long guided American foreign policy. The Trump administration has rolled back programs seeking to promote democracy and human rights.[7] It has shown either neglect or disdain for Africa, and when it has engaged with the continent, it has prioritized an anti-terrorism agenda.[8] This is worrying, but it also presents an unprecedented opportunity for future developments of the Internet, in Africa and globally.

As argued throughout the book, the United States' international politics of the Internet has often been hypocritical. Successive administrations have boasted about the potential of ICTs for freedom and development, and have supported ideas of an open Internet, while spying on users on a global scale,[9] and have failed to act in defense of individuals that have used new media to promote democracy and human rights when they happened to live in countries whose governments were strong US allies.[10]

The heightened tone of the confrontation between supposedly opposite camps, one promoting a free and open Internet, the other a fragmented and authoritarian Internet, have prevented criticism of these practices from reaching a critical mass, contained by the need to take sides in the broader struggle for Internet freedom. As discussed in Chapter 5, in venues such as the WCIT in Dubai, this meant that national and international NGOs, once able to articulate independent positions on the nature of the global information society, uncritically aligned with claims made by the camp led by the United States, without recognizing the contradictions of some of their allies, as well as the merits of alternative positions.

The fact that the Trump administration itself can increasingly be counted among the "enemies of the Internet" for its disregard of net neutrality and support for a corporatist view of the Internet,[11] and that corporate agents that have boasted their credentials as benevolent actors supporting the free and open Internet (e.g. Facebook, Google) have come under increased scrutiny for the model they embrace, is potentially freeing the hands of activists and groups seeking to promote more inclusive ideas of the information society. As has already happened (e.g. before the World Summit for the Information Society), hackers, artists, activists, journalists, and scholars that are critical of what both state and corporate actors are doing can reclaim a position of greater autonomy without being accused of being "agents of the West" or to be simply supporting the position of their funders. This is an uphill task, but, as stressed by Milton Mueller, recognition of the forces that have progressively colonized the Internet, beyond simplistic narratives, can offer a chance for a liberation movement of the Internet to emerge.[12] It would be symbolically very powerful if this movement could develop a strong presence in Africa, evoking its rich history of liberation struggles, and incorporating original thinking on issues of inequalities, discrimination, and communitarianism emerging from the continent.

In 1995, when the first commercial Internet browsers – Netscape and Internet Explorer – had just entered the market, African innovators and policymakers showed remarkable vision, coming together to lay the foundations of what would have become the African Information Society Initiative (AISI), a policy framework aimed at creating a shared "African digital vision."[13] At the time, many of the individuals who contributed ideas to the document had barely had access to the Internet, and AISI was inevitably influenced by the hyped discourses on digital innovation circulating in the 1990s, envisioning transformations that, for the most part, failed to materialize.[14] After having witnessed numerous cycles of promises and failures, hopes and disillusionments, a new initiative for charting Africa's digital future today could have a dramatically different tone, and potentially more radical consequences.

In the past two decades, imageries of Africa and of the Internet seem to have followed opposite trajectories. In 2006, the Kenyan novelist Binyavanga Wainaina wrote a widely popular polemical piece, "How to Write about Africa," where he denounced the stereotypes used to depict the continent as a place with no hope and its people as "too busy starving and dying and warring and emigrating."[15] A few years later, South African journalist Duncan Clarke wrote an almost specular article, "Africa: How to Be an Expert," tracing the emergence of a new set of tropes shaping the narrative of "Africa Rising." This time, talking about Africa required to:

> shed any Afro-pessimism or proclivity for real politik; use terms like "dynamic," "emergent," "middle class" and "last investment frontier" [and stress] unrestricted growth beyond history or capacity: since both are "adjustable," the former by revisionism the latter by "new technology."[16]

Narratives of the Internet, on the contrary, have transitioned from unreserved optimism at the end of the previous millennium (John Perry Barlow's "Declaration of Independence for Cyberspace" became one of the most popular instantiations of this spirit)[17] to concerns the Internet could actually have become a threat to democracy and well-being, reproducing rather than reversing inequalities, promoting hostility rather than empathy towards one another.

Experiencing these dramatic changes in collective mood and perceptions has arguably produced stronger antibodies towards narrations imposed from above, as well as more grounded critical understandings of the realities and potentials of digital innovation. Movements such as #RhodesMustFall and #FeesMustFall have shown the possibility of fresh thinking about ways to redress existing imbalances of power, nationally and internationally. The conditions are ripe to connect the spirit that animated those movements with other visionary projects in the digital realm, such as those aimed at freeing users' data from both corporate and state surveillance, decolonizing digital spaces, and giving power back to individual users.[18] Against rising nationalism, online and offline, demands for a more equitable evolution of the Internet may be able to reactivate the transnational forms of solidarity that once inspired the propagation of the Internet across the globe, inaugurating yet a new phase in the evolution of the information society.

Notes

1 Cass Sunstein, ed., *Can It Happen Here? Authoritarianism in America* (HarperCollins, 2018).

2 Samantha Power, "Beyond Elections: Foreign Interference with American Democracy," in *Can It Happen Here? Authoritarianism in America*, ed. Cass Sunstein (HarperCollins, 2018).

3 Dave Eggers, *The Circle* (Alfred A. Knopf, 2013), 21–22.

4 Charles Rollet, "The Odd Reality of Life under China's All-Seeing Credit Score System," *Wired*, 2018, www.wired.co.uk/article/china-social-credit.

5 Callahan, *China: The Pessoptimist Nation*; Shambaugh, *China Goes Global*; David H. Shinn and Joshua Eisenman, *China and Africa: A Century of Engagement* (University of Pennsylvania Press, 2012); Stephen Chan, *The Morality of China in Africa: The Middle Kingdom and the Dark Continent*, (Zed Books, 2013).

6 Shambaugh, *China Goes Global*; Zheping Huang and Zheping Huang, "China's Huge Celebrations of Karl Marx Are Not Really about Marxism," *Quartz*, 2018, https://qz.com/1270109/chinas-communist-party-and-xi-jinping-are-celebrating-the-200th-birthday-of-karl-marx-with-a-vengeance/.

7 Ted Piccone, "Tillerson Says Goodbye to Human Rights Diplomacy," *Brookings*, May 5, 2017, www.brookings.edu/blog/order-from-chaos/2017/05/05/tillerson-says-goodbye-to-human-rights-diplomacy/.

8 John J. Stremlau, "Three Reasons Why Africa Should Treat Tillerson Visit with Scepticism," *The Conversation*, 2018, http://theconversation.com/three-reasons-why-africa-should-treat-tillerson-visit-with-scepticism-92849; John J. Stremlau, "Trump Should Be the Trigger for Africa to Find Common Cause with Americans," *The Conversation*, 2018, http://theconversation.com/trump-should-be-the-trigger-for-africa-to-find-common-cause-with-americans-93432.

9 Greenwald, *No Place to Hide*.

10 Iginio Gagliardone and Matti Pohjonen, "Engaging in Polarized Society: Social Media and Political Discourse in Ethiopia," in *Digital Activism in the Social Media Era* (Springer International Publishing, 2016), 25–44.

11 Michael J. Coren and Michael J. Coren, "The Senate Just Voted to Reinstate Net Neutrality. Trump and

the House Will Decide Its Fate Now,"
Quartz, 2018, https://qz.com/1280127/
net-neutrality-vote-the-senate-just-
voted-to-overturn-the-the-federal-
communications-commissions-
repeal/; Stremlau, "Trump Should
Be the Trigger for Africa to Find
Common Cause with Americans."

12 Milton Mueller, *Will the
Internet Fragment? Sovereignty,
Globalization and Cyberspace* (John
Wiley & Sons, 2017).

13 UNECA, *The African
Information Society Initiative: A
Decade's Perspective* (UNECA, 2008).

14 For a critical assessment of
the AISI, see Gert Nulens and Leo
Van Audenhove, "An Information
Society in Africa? An Analysis of
the Information Society Policy

ot the World Bank, ITU and
ECA," *Gazette* 61, no. 6 (1999):
451–471; Gagliardone, *The Politics of
Technology in Africa*.

15 Binyavanga Wainaina, "How to
Write about Africa."

16 Duncan Clarke, "Africa: How to
Be an Expert."

17 John Perry Barlow,
"Declaration of Independence for
Cyberspace," (1996), http://wac.
colostate.edu/rhetnet/barlow/
barlow_declaration.html.

18 Kate Clark, "Tim Berners-
Lee Is on a Mission to Decentralize
the Web," *TechCrunch*,
October 9, 2018, http://social.
techcrunch.com/2018/10/09/
tim-berners-lee-is-on-a-mission-to-
decentralize-the-web/.

BIBLIOGRAPHY

Adem, Seifudein. "China in Ethiopia: Diplomacy and Economics of Sino-Optimism." *African Studies Review* 55, no. 1 (April 2012): 143–160. https://doi.org/10.1353/arw.2012.0008.

Alesina, Alberto, and David Dollar. "Who Gives Foreign Aid to Whom and Why?" *Journal of Economic Growth* 5, no. 1 (2000): 33–63.

Allen, Michael, and Gabrielle Hecht. *Technologies of Power: Essays in Honor of Thomas Parke Hughes and Agatha Chipley Hughes.* MIT Press, 2001.

Allen, Tim, and Nicole Stremlau. "Media Policy, Peace and State Reconstruction," 2005. http://eprints.lse.ac.uk/28347/.

Arsène, Séverine. "Global Internet Governance in Chinese Academic Literature: Rebalancing a Hegemonic World Order?" *China Perspectives*, no. 2 (2016): 25.

Asrat, Amare. "Ethiopian, Chinese Parties Agree to Strengthen Relationship." *Fana Broadcasting Corporate*, 2017. www.fanabc.com/english/index.php/news/item/9868-ethiopian,-chinese-parties-agree-to-strengthen-relationship.

AVAAZ. "Click Here to Save the Free Internet!" *AVAAZ*, 2012. https://secure.avaaz.org/en/hands_off_our_internet_i/.

Avgerou, Chrisanthi. *Information Systems and Global Diversity.* Oxford University Press, 2002.

Bachmann, Jan. "Kenya and International Security: Enabling Globalisation, Stabilising 'Stateness', and Deploying Enforcement." *Globalizations* 9, no. 1 (2012): 125–143.

Banda, Fackson. "China in the African Mediascape: A Critical Injection." *Journal of African Media Studies* 1, no. 3 (2009): 343–361.

Barlow, John Perry. "Declaration of Independence for Cyberspace," 1996. http://wac.colostate.edu/rhetnet/barlow/barlow_declaration.html.

Bayart, Jean-François. "Africa in the World: A History of Extraversion." *African Affairs* 99, no. 395 (2000): 217–267.

BBC. "Ethiopia Defends Dissident Arrest." *BBC News*, July 11, 2014, sec. Africa. www.bbc.com/news/world-africa-28272112.

Beall, Jo, Thomas Goodfellow, and James Putzel. "Introductory Article: On the Discourse of Terrorism, Security and Development." *Journal of International Development: The Journal of the Development Studies Association* 18, no. 1 (2006): 51–67.

Bendrath, Ralf, and Milton Mueller. "The End of the Net as We Know It? Deep Packet Inspection and Internet Governance." *New Media & Society* 13, no. 7 (November 1, 2011): 1142–1160. https://doi.org/10.1177/1461444811398031.

Benkler, Yochai, Hal Roberts, Robert Faris, Alicia Solow-Niederman, and Bruce Etling. "Social Mobilization and the Networked Public Sphere: Mapping the SOPA-PIPA Debate." *Political Communication* 32, no. 4 (2015): 594–624.

Berger, Guy. "Problematizing 'Media Development' as a Bandwagon Gets Rolling." *International Communication Gazette* 72, no. 7 (2010): 547–565.

Beyene, Zenebe, Abdissa Zerai, and Iginio Gagliardone. "Satellites, Plasmas and Law: The Role of TeleCourt in Changing Conceptions of Justice and Authority in Ethiopia." *Stability: International Journal of Security and Development* 4, no. 1 (2015). www.stabilityjournal.org/articles/10.5334/sta.fn/.

Bhorat, Haroon, and Finn Tarp. *Africa's Lions: Growth Traps and Opportunities for Six African Economies.* Brookings Institution Press, 2016.

Biset, Blain. "Ethiopia's Anti-Terrorism Law Squelches Opposition, Activists Say." *Inter Press Service*, 2012. www.ipsnews.net/2012/12/ethiopias-anti-terrorism-law-squelches-opposition-activists-say/.

Booth, David, and Frederick Golooba-Mutebi. "Developmental Patrimonialism? The Case of Rwanda." *African Affairs* 111, no. 444 (July 1, 2012): 379–403. https://doi.org/10.1093/afraf/ads026.

Brass, Jennifer. "Kenya's Clampdown on Civil Society Is against Its Self-Interest." *The Conversation*, 2016. http://theconversation.com/kenyas-clampdown-on-civil-society-is-against-its-self-interest-62019.

Brautigam, Deborah. "Aid 'With Chinese Characteristics': Chinese Foreign Aid and Development Finance Meet the OECD-DAC Aid Regime." *Journal of International Development* 23, no. 5 (2011): 752–764.

——. "Ethiopia's Partnership with China." *The Guardian*, December 30, 2011. www.theguardian.com/global-development/poverty-matters/2011/dec/30/china-ethiopia-business-opportunities.

Brisset-Foucault, Florence. "Radio, Mobile Phones, Elite Formation and Sociability: The Case of Uganda's 'Serial Callers,'" 2013. https://papers.ssrn.com/sol3/papers.cfm?abstract_id=2250539.

Brooks, Jermyn. "Opinion: Hands off the Internet!" *The New York Times*, December 6, 2012, sec. Opinion. www.nytimes.com/2012/12/07/opinion/hands-off-the-internet.html.

Brown, Stephen, and Jörn Grävingholt. *The Securitization of Foreign Aid.* Springer, 2016.

Bughin, Jacques. *Lions on the Move II: Realizing the Potential of Africa's Economies.* McKinsey Global Institute, 2016.

Burrell, Jenna. *Invisible Users: Youth in the Internet Cafés of Urban Ghana.* MIT Press, 2012.

Callahan, William A. *China: The Pessoptimist Nation.* Oxford University Press, 2009.

Carmody, Pádraig, and Ian Taylor. "Flexigemony and Force in China's Resource Diplomacy in Africa: Sudan and Zambia Compared." *Geopolitics* 15, no. 3 (2010): 496–515.

Chan, Stephen. *The Morality of China in Africa: The Middle Kingdom and the Dark Continent.* Zed Books, 2013.

Chandler, David. "The Security–Development Nexus and the Rise of 'Anti-Foreign Policy.'" *Journal of International Relations and Development* 10, no. 4 (2007): 362–386.

Cherian, Samuel. "Asian Participation in the London Process." *Institute for Defence Studies and Analyses*, March 31, 2015. https://idsa.in/idsacomments/AsianParticipationintheLondonProcess%2520_csamuel_310315.

Cheung, Anne SY. "Exercising Freedom of Speech behind the Great Firewall: A Study of Judges' and Lawyers' Blogs in China." *Harvard International Law Journal Online* 52, no. 250 (2011). http://papers.ssrn.com/sol3/papers.cfm?abstract_id=1844003.

China Daily. "China Daily Launches Africa Weekly Edition." *China Daily*, December 14, 2012. www.chinadaily.com.cn/china/2012-12/14/content_16016334.htm.

China's Second Africa Policy Paper. www.chinadaily.com.cn/world/XiattendsParisclimateconference/2015-12/05/content_22632874.htm.

Clark, Kate. "Tim Berners-Lee Is on a Mission to Decentralize the Web." *TechCrunch*, October 9, 2018. http://social.techcrunch.com/2018/10/09/tim-berners-lee-is-on-a-mission-to-decentralize-the-web/.

Clarke, Duncan. "Africa: How to Be an Expert." *The Guardian*, November 12, 2012, sec. World News. www.theguardian.com/world/2012/nov/12/africa-expert-celebrity-madonna.

Clinton, Bill. "Full Text of Clinton's Speech on China Trade Bill." *The New York Times*, March 9, 2000. https://partners.nytimes.com/library/world/asia/030900clinton-china-text.html?mcubz=0.

Clinton, Hillary. "Remarks on Internet Freedom." *US Department of State*, January 21, 2010.

www.state.gov/secretary/
rm/2010/01/135519.htm.

Cook, Sarah. "The Long Shadow
of Chinese Censorship," 2013.
http://ignucius.bd.ub.es:8180/
jspui/handle/123456789/787.

Coren, Michael J., and Michael J.
Coren. "The Senate Just Voted
to Reinstate Net Neutrality.
Trump and the House Will
Decide Its Fate Now." *Quartz*,
2018. https://qz.com/1280127/
net-neutrality-vote-the-senate-
just-voted-to-overturn-the-
the-federal-communications-
commissions-repeal/.

Crabtree, Justina. "'China Is
Everywhere' in Africa's
Rising Technology Industry."
CNBC, July 28, 2017. www.
cnbc.com/2017/07/28/
china-is-everywhere-in-
africas-rising-technology-
industry.html.

Creemers, Rogier. "Cyber China:
Upgrading Propaganda, Public
Opinion Work and Social
Management for the Twenty-
First Century." *Journal of
Contemporary China*, 26, no. 103
(2017): 85–100.

_____. "The Privilege of Speech and
New Media: Conceptualizing
China's Communications Law in
the Internet Era," 2014. http://
papers.ssrn.com/sol3/papers.
cfm?abstract_id=2379959.

DAC. "A Development Co-Operation
Lens on Terrorism Prevention:
Key Entry Points for Action."
DAC High Level Meeting, 2003.

Dalton, Matthew. "Telecom Deal by
China's ZTE, Huawei in Ethiopia
Faces Criticism." *Wall Street
Journal*, January 7, 2014, sec.
World. http://online.wsj.com/
news/articles/SB1000142405270
2303653004579212092223818288.

Deibert, Ronald, John Palfrey, Rafal
Rohozinski, and Jonathan
Zittrain. *Access Contested:
Security, Identity, and Resistance
in Asian Cyberspace.*
MIT Press, 2012.

_____. *Access Controlled: The Shaping
of Power, Rights, and Rule in
Cyberspace.* MIT Press, 2010.

_____. *Access Denied: The Practice
and Policy of Global Internet
Filtering.* MIT Press, 2008.

Dreher, Axel, and Andreas Fuchs.
"Rogue Aid? The Determinants of
China's Aid Allocation." *Courant
Research Centre: Poverty,
Equity and Growth-Discussion
Papers*, 2011. www.econstor.eu/
handle/10419/90522.

Driessen, Miriam. "The African
Bill: Chinese Struggles with
Development Assistance."
Anthropology Today 31, no. 1
(2015): 3–7.

Du, Shanshan. "Social Media and
the Transformation of 'Chinese
Nationalism': 'Igniting Positive
Energy' in China since the 2012
London Olympics." *Anthropology
Today* 30, no. 1 (2014): 5–8.

Duffield, Mark. *Development,
Security and Unending War:
Governing the World of Peoples.*
Polity, 2007.

Economy, Elizabeth C. "The Great Firewall of China: Xi Jinping's Internet Shutdown." *The Guardian*, June 29, 2018, sec. News. www.theguardian. com/news/2018/jun/29/ the-great-firewall-of-china-xi-jinpings-internet-shutdown

Eggers, Dave. *The Circle*. Alfred A. Knopf, 2013.

Evans, Peter. *Embedded Autonomy: States and Industrial Transformation*. Princeton University Press, 1995.

Farah, Douglas, and Andy Mosher. *Winds from the East*. Center for International Media Assistance, 2010.

Farrell, Henry, and Martha Finnemore. "The End of Hypocrisy: American Foreign Policy in the Age of Leaks." *Foreign Affairs* 92, no. 6 (2013): 22–26.

Fisher, Jonathan, and David M. Anderson. "Authoritarianism and the Securitization of Development in Africa." *International Affairs* 91, no. 1 (2015): 131–151.

Fortin, Jacey. "Ethiopia: Bloggers and Journalists Are Charged as Terrorists." *The New York Times*, July 18, 2014. www. nytimes.com/2014/07/19/world/ africa/ethiopia-bloggers-and-journalists-are-charged-as-terrorists.html

Forum on China-Africa Cooperation. *Beijing Action Plan (2007–2009)*. www.fmprc.gov.cn/zflt/eng/zyzl/ hywj/t280369.htm.

Foster, Vivien, and Cecilia Briceño-Garmendia. *Africa Infrastructure Country Diagnostic*. World Bank, 2009. www.energytoolbox. org/library/infra2008/ references/34_12-17-08_africas_ infrastructure_foster.pdf.

Fourie, Elsje. *New Maps for Africa? Contextualising the "Chinese Model" within Ethiopian and Kenyan Paradigms of Development*. University of Trento, 2013.

French, Howard W. *China's Second Continent: How a Million Migrants Are Building a New Empire in Africa*. Vintage, 2014.

Friedberg, Aaron L. *"Going Out": China's Pursuit of Natural Resources and Implications for the PRC's Grand Strategy*. Vol. 17, 3. National Bureau of Asian Research, 2006. www.ou.edu/uschina/ SASD/SASD2007readings/ Friedberg2006GoingOut.pdf.

Fu, Xiaolan. "Foreign Direct Investment, Absorptive Capacity and Regional Innovation Capabilities: Evidence from China." *Oxford Development Studies* 36, no. 1 (2008): 89–110.

Fu, Xiaolan, Carlo Pietrobelli, and Luc Soete. "The Role of Foreign Technology and Indigenous Innovation in the Emerging Economies: Technological Change and Catching-Up." *World Development* 39, no. 7 (2011): 1204–1212.

Furzey, Jane. "A Critical Examination of the Social, Economic, Technical and Policy Issues, with Respect to the Expansion or Initiation of Information and Communications Infrastructure in Ethiopia." Empowering Socio-Economic Development in Africa Utilizing Information Technology, 1995.

Gadzala, Aleksandra W. *Africa and China: How Africans and Their Governments Are Shaping Relations with China.* Rowman & Littlefield, 2015.

Gagliardone, Iginio. "'Can You Hear Me?' Mobile–Radio Interactions and Governance in Africa." *New Media & Society* 18, no. 9 (2016): 2080–2095.

_____. "China and the African Internet: Perspectives from Kenya and Ethiopia/China y El Internet Africano: Perspectivas Desde Kenia y Etiopía." *Index. Comunicación* 3, no. 2 (2013): 67–82.

_____. "China as a Persuader: CCTV Africa's First Steps in the African Mediasphere." *Ecquid Novi: African Journalism Studies* 34, no. 3 (2013): 25–40.

_____. "From Mapping Information Ecologies to Evaluating Media Interventions: An Experts Survey on Evaluating Media Interventions in Conflict Countries." Report published by United States Institute of Peace (USIP). Washington, DC, 2010.

_____. "Media Development with Chinese Characteristics." *Global Media Journal* 4, no. 2 (2014): 1–16.

_____. *The Politics of Technology in Africa.* Cambridge University Press, 2016.

Gagliardone, Iginio, and Frederick Golooba-Mutebi. "The Evolution of the Internet in Ethiopia and Rwanda: Towards a 'Developmental' Model?" *Stability: International Journal of Security and Development* 5, no. 1 (2016). www.stabilityjournal.org/articles/10.5334/sta.344/.

Gagliardone, Iginio, and Pál Nyíri. "Freer but Not Free Enough? Chinese Journalists Finding Their Feet in Africa." *Journalism* 18, no. 8 (2017): 1049–1063.

Gagliardone, Iginio, and Matti Pohjonen. "Engaging in Polarized Society: Social Media and Political Discourse in Ethiopia." In *Digital Activism in the Social Media Era*, 25–44. Springer International Publishing, 2016.

Gagliardone, Iginio, Maria Repnikova, and Nicole Stremlau. "China in Africa: A New Approach to Media Development?" Oxford, 2010. https://global.asc.upenn.edu/publications/china-in-africa-a-new-approach-to-media-development/.

Gagliardone, Iginio, Nicole Stremlau, and Daniel Nkrumah. "Partner, Prototype or Persuader? China's Renewed Media Engagement with Ghana." *Communication,*

Politics & Culture 45, no. 2
(2012). http://mams.rmit.edu.au/
xb03w37se3t8z.pdf.

Gao, Ping, and Kalle Lyytinen.
"Transformation of China's
Telecommunications Sector:
A Macro Perspective."
Telecommunications Policy 24,
no. 8 (2000): 719–730.

Geall, Sam, ed. *China and the
Environment: The Green
Revolution.* Zed Books, 2013.

GhanaWeb. "Shutdown Social
Media if Necessary –
Group." *GhanaWeb*, 2016.
www.ghanaweb.com/
GhanaHomePage/NewsArchive/
Shutdown-social-media-if-
necessary-Group-443682.

Goldsmith, Jack L., and Tim Wu. *Who
Controls the Internet? Illusions
of a Borderless World.* Oxford
University Press, 2006. http://
jost.syr.edu/wp-content/uploads/
who-controls-the-internet_
illusions-of-a-borderless-
world.pdf.

Gordon, Robert J. *The Rise and Fall
of American Growth: The US
Standard of Living since the
Civil War.* Vol. 70. Princeton
University Press, 2017.

Government of Ethiopia.
"Information Network Security
Agency Re-Establishment
Proclamation No. 808/2013,"
2013.

———. "Proclamation No. 652/2009 of
2009, Anti-Terrorism Proclamation
(2009)." www.refworld.org/
docid/4ba799d32.html.

Government of Rwanda. "An
Integrated ICT-Led Socio-
Economic Development Plan
for Rwanda." *GESCI*, 2010. www.
gesci.org/old/files/docman/
NICIfinal2.pdf.

Government of the United Kingdom.
Terrorism Act 2006 (2006).
www.legislation.gov.uk/
ukpga/2006/11/section/1.

Greenwald, Glenn. *No Place to Hide.*
Penguin, 2014.

Griffith, Patrick. "Ethiopia's Anti-
Terrorism Proclamation and
the Right to Freedom of
Expression." *Freedom Now*,
2013. www.freedom-now.org/
news/ethiopias-anti-terrorism-
proclamation-and-the-right-to-
freedom-of-expression/.

Groves, Jason. "Cameron Warns
Africans over the 'Chinese
Invasion' as They Pour Billions
into Continent." *Daily Mail*, July
19, 2011. www.dailymail.co.uk/
news/article-2016677/Cameron-
warns-Africans-Chinese-
invasion-pour-billions-continent.
html.

Gurstein, Michael. "Civil Society and
the Emerging Internet Cold War:
Non-Alignment and the Public
Interest." *Gurstein's Community
Informatics*, February 11, 2013.
https://gurstein.wordpress.
com/2013/02/11/civil-society-
and-the-emerging-internet-cold-
war-non-alignment-and-the-
public-interest/.

———. "Networking the Networked/
Closing the Loop: Some Notes

on WSIS II," 2005. www. worldsummit2003.de/en/ web/847.htm.

_____. "(Whose) Hands off (What) Internet? Some Reflections on WCIT 2012." *Gurstein's Community Informatics*, 2012. http://gurstein. wordpress.com/2012/12/09/ whose-hand-off-what-internet-some-reflections-on-wcit-2012/.

Haas, Benjamin. "China Moves to Block Internet VPNs from 2018." *The Guardian*, July 11, 2017. www. theguardian.com/world/2017/ jul/11/china-moves-to-block-internet-vpns-from-2018.

Hallin, Daniel C., and Paolo Mancini. *Comparing Media Systems beyond the Western World*. Cambridge University Press, 2011.

Hallin, Daniel, and Paolo Mancini. *Comparing Media Systems: Three Models of Media and Politics*. Cambridge University Press, 2004.

Hassid, Jonathan. "Controlling the Chinese Media: An Uncertain Business." *University of California, Reprinted from Asian Survey* 48, no. 3 (2008): 414–430.

He, Baogang, and Mark E. Warren. "Authoritarian Deliberation: The Deliberative Turn in Chinese Political Development." *Perspectives on Politics* 9, no. 2 (2011): 269–289.

Headley, James. "Challenging the EU's Claim to Moral Authority: Russian Talk of 'Double Standards.'" *Asia Europe Journal* 13, no. 3 (2015): 297–307.

Heever, Claire van den. "Huawei's Quest for Hearts and Minds in Africa." *Asia Times*, 2016. www. atimes.com/article/huaweis-quest-hearts-minds-africa/.

Hindman, Matthew. *The Myth of Digital Democracy*. Princeton University Press, 2008.

Hintz, Arne. "Deconstructing Multi-Stakeholderism: The Discourses and Realities of Global Governance at the World Summit on the Information Society (WSIS)." In *SGIR Pan-European International Relations Conference*, 2007. www.eisa-net.org/be-bruga/eisa/files/ events/turin/hintz-sgir_ahintz_ deconstructing.pdf.

Hoeffler, Anke, and Verity Outram. "Need, Merit, or Self-Interest: What Determines the Allocation of Aid?" *Review of Development Economics* 15, no. 2 (2011): 237–250.

Howell, Jude, and Jeremy Lind. *Counter-Terrorism, Aid and Civil Society: Before and after the War on Terror*. Palgrave Macmillan, 2009.

Huang, Zheping. "China's Huge Celebrations of Karl Marx Are Not Really about Marxism." *Quartz*, 2018. https://qz.com/1270109/ chinas-communist-party-and-xi-jinping-are-celebrating-the-200th-birthday-of-karl-marx-with-a-vengeance/.

Hughes, Nick, and Susie Lonie. "M-PESA: Mobile Money for the 'Unbanked' Turning Cellphones into 24-Hour Tellers in Kenya." *Innovations* 2, no. 1–2 (2007): 63–81.

Hughes, Thomas P. *Networks of Power: Electrification in Western Society, 1880–1930.* Johns Hopkins University Press, 1983.

Human Rights Watch. "Ethiopia: Terrorism Law Decimates Media." *Human Rights Watch*, May 3, 2013. www.hrw.org/news/2013/05/03/ethiopia-terrorism-law-decimates-media.

Hyun, Ki Deuk, and Jinhee Kim. "The Role of New Media in Sustaining the Status Quo: Online Political Expression, Nationalism, and System Support in China." *Information, Communication & Society* 18, no. 7 (2015): 766–781.

Hyun, Ki Deuk, Jinhee Kim, and Shaojing Sun. "News Use, Nationalism, and Internet Use Motivations as Predictors of Anti-Japanese Political Actions in China." *Asian Journal of Communication* 24, no. 6 (2014): 589–604.

Igihe. "Ethiopia, Rwanda Discuss Commodity Exchange," 2011. http://business/ethiopia-rwanda-discuss-commodity-exchange.html.

iHub Research. "Umati Final Report." Nairobi, Kenya, 2013. www.research.ihub.co.ke/uploads/2013/june/1372415606_936.pdf.

Inkster, Nigel. "Battle for the Soul of the Internet." *Adelphi Series* 55, no. 456 (2015): 109–142.

International Commission of Jurists. "Assessing Damage, Urging Action: Report of the Eminent Jurists Panel on Terrorism, Counter-Terrorism and Human Rights." Geneva, 2009.

ITU. *Key ICT Indicators for Developed and Developing Countries and the World.* www.itu.int/en/ITU-D/Statistics/Documents/statistics/2018/ITU_Key_2005-2018_ICT_data_with%20LDCs_rev27Nov2018.xls.

Jiang, Min. "Authoritarian Deliberation on Chinese Internet." *Electronic Journal of Communication* 20 (2009). http://papers.ssrn.com/sol3/papers.cfm?abstract_id=1439354.

Jinping, Xi. "Remarks by H.E. Xi Jinping President of the People's Republic of China at the Opening Ceremony of the Second World Internet Conference." *Ministry of Foreign Affairs of the People's Republic of China*, 2015. www.fmprc.gov.cn/mfa_eng/wjdt_665385/zyjh_665391/t1327570.shtml.

Jones, Will, Ricardo Soares de Oliveira, and Harry Verhoeven. *Africa's Illiberal State-Builders.* Refugee Studies Centre, 2012.

Kabweza. "Chinese Style Internet Censorship Coming to Zimbabwe – President Mugabe." *Techzim*, April 4, 2016. www.techzim.co.zw/2016/04/china-style-internet-censorship-coming-to-zimbabwe-president-mugabe/.

Kalathil, Shanthi. "Scaling a Changing Curve: Traditional Media Development and the New Media." *CIMA*, 2008. http://cima.ned.org/publications/research-reports/scaling-changing-curve-traditional-media-development-and-new-media#sthash.s3rzgycq.dpuf.

Kanter, James. "E.U., Citing Amazon and Apple, Tells Nations to Collect Tax." *The New York Times*, October 4, 2017, sec. Business Day. www.nytimes.com/2017/10/04/business/eu-tax-amazon-apple.html.

Kanyesigye, Frank. "Local Govt Leaders Upbeat after Inaugural Video Conference." *The New Times Rwanda*, 2013. www.newtimes.co.rw/section/read/70087/.

Kassa, Wondwossen Demissie. "Examining Some of the Raisons D'Etre for the Ethiopian Anti-Terrorism Law." *Mizan Law Review* 7, no. 1 (2014). www.ajol.info/index.php/mlr/article/view/100534.

Kelsall, Tim. *Business, Politics and the State in Africa: Challenging the Orthodoxies on Growth and Transformation*. Zed Books, 2013.

King, Gary, Jennifer Pan, and Margaret E. Roberts. "How Censorship in China Allows Government Criticism but Silences Collective Expression." *American Political Science Review* 107, no. 2 (2013): 326–343.

King, Kenneth. *China's Aid and Soft Power in Africa: The Case of Education and Training*. James Currey, 2013.

Kiyokazu, Koshida. "Militarization of Japan ODA." *Reality of Aid*, 2004. www.realityofaid.org/wp-content/uploads/2013/02/2004Oct_security-agenda-and-development.pdf.

Kleine-Ahlbrandt, Stephanie, and Andrew Small. "China's New Dictatorship Diplomacy: Is Beijing Parting with Pariahs?" *Foreign Affairs* 87, no. 1 (2008): 38–56.

Klimburg, Alexander. "The Internet Yalta." *Center for a New American Security*, 2013, 2.

Kluver, Randolph, and Chen Yang. "The Internet in China: A Meta-Review of Research." *The Information Society* 21, no. 4 (2005): 301–308.

Krause-Jackson, Flavia. "Clinton Chastises China on Internet, African 'New Colonialism.'" *Bloomberg*, June 11, 2011. www.bloomberg.com/news/articles/2011-06-11/clinton-chastises-china-on-internet-african-new-colonialism-.

Kumar, Krishna. "International Assistance to Promote Independent Media in Transition and Post-Conflict Societies." *Democratization* 13, no. 4 (2006): 652–667.

Kuo, Lily. "Why Is China Investing So Heavily in a Small Landlocked African Country with Few Natural Resources?" *Quartz*, 2017. https://qz.com/827935/rwanda-is-a-landlocked-country-with-few-natural-resources-so-why-is-china-investing-so-heavily-in-it/.

Kurlantzick, Joshua. *Charm Offensive: How China's Soft Power Is Transforming the World.* Yale University Press, 2007.

Lagerkvist, Johan. *After the Internet, before Democracy: Competing Norms in Chinese Media and Society.* Peter Lang, 2010.

_____. "Chinese Eyes on Africa: Authoritarian Flexibility versus Democratic Governance." *Journal of Contemporary African Studies* 27, no. 2 (2009): 119–134.

Lakoff, George. *The All New Don't Think of an Elephant! Know Your Values and Frame the Debate.* Chelsea Green Publishing, 2014.

Lam, Willy. "Chinese State Media Goes Global: A Great Leap Outward for Chinese Soft Power?" *China Brief* 9, no. 2 (2009): 2–4.

Lancaster, Henry. "Kenya: Telecoms, Mobile, and Broadband." Budde, 2015.

_____. "Rwanda: Telecoms, Mobile, and Broadband." Budde, 2015.

Lekorwe, Mogopodi, Anyway Chingwete, Mina Okuru, and Romaric Samson. "China's Growing Presence in Africa Wins Largely Positive Popular Reviews." *Afrobarometer*, 2016. http://afrobarometer.org/publications/wp117-african-perspectives-china-africa-gauging-popular-perceptions-and-their-economic.

Leonard, Mark. *What Does China Think?* Fourth Estate, 2008.

Lessig, Lawrence. *Code: And Other Laws of Cyberspace.* ReadHowYouWant, 2009.

Llanso, Emma, and Alissa Cooper. "Adoption of Traffic Sniffing Standard Fans WCIT Flames." *Center for Democracy & Technology*, 2012. https://cdt.org/blog/adoption-of-traffic-sniffing-standard-fans-wcit-flames/.

Maasho, Aaron. "China Denies Report It Hacked African Union Headquarters." *Reuters*, January 29, 2018. www.reuters.com/article/us-africanunion-summit-china/china-denies-report-it-hacked-african-union-headquarters-idUSKBN1FI2I5.

_____. "Ethiopia Charges Nine Bloggers, Journalists with Inciting Violence." *Reuters*. April 28, 2014. www.reuters.com/article/2014/04/28/us-ethiopia-politics-idUSBREA3R0YC20140428.

MacKinnon, Rebecca. "Cyber Zone." *Index on Censorship* 37, no. 2 (2008): 82–89.

Madrid-Morales, Dani, and Herman Wasserman. "Chinese Media Engagement in South Africa:

What Is Its Impact on Local Journalism?" *Journalism Studies*, 2017, 1–18.

Mann, Laura, and Elie Nzayisenga. "Sellers on the Street: The Human Infrastructure of the Mobile Phone Network in Kigali, Rwanda." *Critical African Studies* 7, no. 1 (2015): 26–46.

Marsh, Vivien. "Chinese State Television's 'Going Out' Strategy: A True Global News Contraflow? A Comparison of News on CCTV's Africa Live and BBC World News TV's Focus on Africa." China's Soft Power in Africa: Emerging Media and Cultural Relations between China and Africa. Nottingham University's Ningbo Campus, 2014.

_____. "Mixed Messages, Partial Pictures? Discourses under Construction in CCTV's Africa Live Compared with the BBC." *Chinese Journal of Communication* 9, no. 1 (2016): 56–70.

McConnon, Eamonn. "Fighting Poverty to Fight Terrorism: Security in DFID's Development Policy during the War on Terror." *Forum for Development Studies* 41 (2014): 135–157.

McKune, Sarah. "Analysis of International Code of Conduct." *The Citizen Lab*, September 28, 2015. https://citizenlab.ca/2015/09/international-code-of-conduct/.

Menkhaus, Ken. *Somalia: State Collapse and the Threat of Terrorism*. Routledge, 2013.

_____. "The Crisis in Somalia: Tragedy in Five Acts." *African Affairs* 106, no. 424 (2007): 357–390.

Mohan, Giles, and Ben Lampert. "Negotiating China: Reinserting African Agency into China–Africa Relations." *African Affairs* 112, no. 446 (2013): 92–110.

Moody, Glyn. "ITU Approves Deep Packet Inspection Standard Behind Closed Doors, Ignores Huge Privacy Implications." *Techdirt*, 2012. www.techdirt.com/articles/20121203/07493221209/itu-approves-deep-packet-inspection-standard-behind-closed-doors-ignores-huge-privacy-implications.shtml.

Morawczynski, Olga. "Exploring the Usage and Impact of 'Transformational' Mobile Financial Services: The Case of M-PESA in Kenya." *Journal of Eastern African Studies* 3, no. 3 (2009): 509–525.

Morozov, Evgeny. *The Net Delusion: The Dark Side of Internet Freedom*. PublicAffairs, 2012.

Moss, Todd, and Sarah Rose. "China ExIm Bank and Africa: New Lending, New Challenges." *CGD Notes*, 2006. http://mercury.ethz.ch/serviceengine/Files/ISN/38231/ipublicationdocument_singledocument/12344342-ee55-4679-8955-d27614b78bf4/en/2006_11_06.pdf.

Mueller, Milton. *China in the Information Age: Telecommunications and the Dilemmas of Reform.* Greenwood Publishing Group, 1997.

———. *Network and States: The Global Politics of Internet Governance.* MIT Press, 2010.

———. "What Really Happened in Dubai?" *Internet Governance Project*, December 13, 2012. www.internetgovernance. org/2012/12/13/what-really-happened-in-dubai/.

———. *Will the Internet Fragment? Sovereignty, Globalization and Cyberspace.* John Wiley & Sons, 2017.

Myers, Mary. "Donor Support for Media Development." In *Whose Voices? Media and Pluralism in the Context of Democratisation*, edited by L. Rudebeck and M. Melin. University of Uppsala, 2008.

Ndubuisi, Francis. "FG, China Exim Bank Seal $600m Deal on Abuja Light Rail, Galaxy Backbone." *This Day Live*, September 13, 2012. www.thisdaylive.com/ articles/ fg-china-exim-bank-seal-600m-deal-on-abuja-light-railgalaxy- backbone/124857.

Nicola, Stefan, and Birgit Jennen. "Germany Gets Really Serious About Fake News on Facebook." *Bloomberg*, April 5, 2017. www.bloomberg.com/news/ articles/2017-04-05/merkel-cabinet-backs-facebook-fines-to-stem-fake-news-in-germany.

"Nigeria's Space Program: A Rare Glimpse Inside the West African Nation's Satellite Operation." *International Business Times.* www.ibtimes.com/nigerias-space-program-rare-glimpse-inside-west-african-nations-satellite-operation-1411236.

NITA. "President Inaugurates a $38 Million Fiber Optic Backbone Project." *NITA*, 2015. http:// nita.gov.gh/article/president-inaugurates-38-million-fiber-optic-backbone-project.

Noesselt, Nele. "Microblogs and the Adaptation of the Chinese Party-State's Governance Strategy." *Governance* 27, no. 3 (2014): 449–468.

Nonnecke, Brandie M. "The Transformative Effects of Multistakeholderism in Internet Governance: A Case Study of the East Africa Internet Governance Forum." *Telecommunications Policy* 40, no. 4 (2016): 343–352.

Nulens, Gert, and Leo Van Audenhove. "An Information Society in Africa? An Analysis of the Information Society Policy of the World Bank, ITU and ECA." *Gazette* 61, no. 6 (1999): 451–471.

Nye, Joseph. "Why China Is Weak on Soft Power." *The New York Times*, January 17, 2012, sec. Opinion. www.nytimes.com/2012/01/18/ opinion/why-china-is-weak-on-soft-power.html.

Okuttah, Mark. "Safaricom Loosens China's Grip on Local Contracts with Sh14bn Tender." *Business*

Daily, December 6, 2012. www.businessdailyafrica. com/Corporate-News/ Safaricom-loosens-China-grip-on-local-contracts/-/539550/1638364/-/11xotu6z/-/index.html.

———. "Telkom Kenya Set to Run Fibre Network on Behalf of Government." *Business Daily*, June 1, 2010. www.businessdailyafrica. com/Corporate-News/ Telkom-Kenya-set-to-run-fibre-network-on-behalf-of-government/-/539550/929626/-/m96mry/-/index.html.

Olander, Eric. "Why China Is Pushing Back So Hard against Spying Accusations in Africa," February 17, 2018, www.youtube.com/watch?v=ntwa9iKJ85M.

Padovani, Claudia, and Elena Pavan. "Diversity Reconsidered in a Global Multi-Stakeholder Environment: Insights from the Online World." In *The Power of Ideas: Internet Governance in a Global Multistakeholder Environment*, edited by Wolfgang Kleinwachter. Marketing for Deutschland, 2007.

Pearce, Katy E., and Sarah Kendzior. "Networked Authoritarianism and Social Media in Azerbaijan." *Journal of Communication* 62, no. 2 (2012): 283–298.

Pew Research Center. "Global Indicators Database." *Pew Research Center's Global Attitudes Project*, 2017. www. pewglobal.org/database/.

Piccone, Ted. "Tillerson Says Goodbye to Human Rights Diplomacy." *Brookings*, May 5, 2017. www.brookings.edu/blog/order-from-chaos/2017/05/05/tillerson-says-goodbye-to-human-rights-diplomacy/.

Pinch, Trevor J., Malcolm Ashmore, and Michael Mulkay. "Technology, Testing, Text: Clinical Budgeting in the UK National Health Service." In *Shaping Technology/Building Society: Studies in Sociotechnical Change*, edited by Wiebe E. Bijker and John Law. MIT Press, 1992.

Pollpeter, Kevin. *Building for the Future: China's Progress in Space Technology during the Tenth 5-Year Plan and the US Response.* Maroon Ebooks, 2015.

Power, Samantha. "Beyond Elections: Foreign Interference with American Democracy." In *Can It Happen Here? Authoritarianism in America*, edited by Cass Sunstein. HarperCollins, 2018.

Purdeková, Andrea. "'Even if I Am Not Here, There Are so Many Eyes': Surveillance and State Reach in Rwanda." *The Journal of Modern African Studies* 49, no. 3 (2011): 475–497.

Qiu, Jack Linchuan. "Goodbye ISlave: Foxconn, Digital Capitalism, and Networked Labor Resistance." *Society: Chinese Journal of Sociology/Shehui* 34, no. 4 (2014).

Qiu, Jack Linchuan, and Wei Bu. "China ICT Studies: A Review of the Field, 1989–2012." *China Review* 13, no. 2 (2013): 123–152.

Raboy, Marc, and Claudia Padovani. "Mapping Global Media Policy: Concepts, Frameworks, Methods." *Communication, Culture & Critique* 3, no. 2 (2010): 150–169.

Reporters Without Borders. "China: World's Leading Prison for Citizen Journalists," 2017. https://rsf.org/en/china.

———. "Enemies of the Internet," 2014. http://12mars.rsf.org/2014-en/.

Reuters. "Uganda Blocks Social Media, Clamps Down Before President Sworn In." *Reuters*, May 12, 2016. https://af.reuters.com/article/africaTech/idAFKCN0Y30YC.

Rid, Thomas. "Snowden, 多谢 多谢 | Kings of War," 2014. http://kingsofwar.org.uk/2014/03/snowden-thanks-very-much/.

Rollet, Charles. "The Odd Reality of Life under China's All-Seeing Credit Score System." *Wired*, 2018. www.wired.co.uk/article/china-social-credit.

Rugonzibwa, Pius. "Tanzania: China Aid to Boost National Budget." *Tanzania Daily News*, March 27, 2013. http://allafrica.com/stories/201303270063.html.

Sackitey, Francis. "Huawei Nudges Ghana to E-Government." *This Is Africa*, 2013. www.thisisafricaonline.com/Development/Huawei-nudges-Ghana-to-e-government.

Salidjanova, Nargiza, US-China Economic, Security Review Commission, and others. *Going Out: An Overview of China's Outward Foreign Direct Investment*. US-China Economic and Security Review Commission, 2011. www.bioin.or.kr/InnoDS/data/upload/policy/1314079084656.pdf.

Saliu, Olatunji, and Zhang Baoping. "China Initiates Satellite TV Project in Rural Africa," 2017. http://news.xinhuanet.com/english/2017-08/11/c_136517844.htm.

Schmidt, Eric, and Jared Cohen. *The New Digital Age: Reshaping the Future of People, Nations and Business*. Random House, 2013.

Shaban, Hamza. "Former Google Chief Predicts the Internet Will Split by 2028: A Chinese Web and an American One." *Washington Post*, 2018. www.washingtonpost.com/technology/2018/09/21/former-google-chief-predicts-internet-will-split-by-chinese-web-an-american-one/.

Shambaugh, David L. *China Goes Global: The Partial Power*. Oxford University Press, 2013.

Shen, Hong. "China and Global Internet Governance: Toward an Alternative Analytical Framework." *Chinese Journal of Communication* 9, no. 3 (July 2, 2016): 304–324. https://doi.org/10.1080/17544750.2016.1206028.

Shinn, David H., and Joshua Eisenman. *China and Africa: A Century of Engagement.* University of Pennsylvania Press, 2012.

Simone, AbdouMaliq. "People as Infrastructure: Intersecting Fragments in Johannesburg." *Public Culture* 16, no. 3 (2004): 407–429.

Somerville, Keith. "Violence, Hate Speech and Inflammatory Broadcasting in Kenya: The Problems of Definition and Identification." *Ecquid Novi: African Journalism Studies* 32, no. 1 (2011): 82–101.

"SOPA and PIPA Bills Lose Support on Capitol Hill as Google, Wikipedia and Others Stage Protests." *Washington Post*, January 18, 2012, sec. Business. www.washingtonpost.com/business/economy/sopa-and-pipa-bills-lose-support-on-capitol-hill-as-google-wikipedia-and-others-stage-protests/2012/01/18/gIQAwls38P_story.html.

State Council of the People's Republic of China. "The Internet in China. White Paper," June 8, 2010. www.china.org.cn/government/whitepaper/node_7093508.htm.

Stephen. "Chinese Rocket Launches Powerful Nigerian Satellite into Orbit." *Space*. www.space.com/13975-china-rocket-launching-huge-nigeria-satellite.html.

Stremlau, John J. "Three Reasons Why Africa Should Treat Tillerson Visit with Scepticism." *The Conversation*, 2018. http://theconversation.com/three-reasons-why-africa-should-treat-tillerson-visit-with-scepticism-92849.

_____. "Trump Should Be the Trigger for Africa to Find Common Cause with Americans." *The Conversation*, 2018. http://theconversation.com/trump-should-be-the-trigger-for-africa-to-find-common-cause-with-americans-93432.

Stremlau, Nicole. *The Press and Consolidation of Power in Ethiopia and Uganda.* PhD thesis, London School of Economics and Political Science, 2008. http://etheses.lse.ac.uk/2160/2008.

Sun, Yun. "Africa in China's Foreign Policy." Brookings, 2014. www.wlv.ac.uk/media/departments/faculty-of-social-sciences/documents/Africa_in_China_Brookings_report.pdf.

Sunstein, Cass, ed. *Can It Happen Here? Authoritarianism in America.* HarperCollins, 2018.

Tan-Mullins, May, Giles Mohan, and Marcus Power. "Redefining 'Aid' in the China–Africa Context." *Development and Change* 41, no. 5 (2010): 857–881.

TeleGeography. "Huawei Bags Guinean Backbone Contract, Sotelgui Rescue Plans Ongoing." *TeleGeography*, 2013.

www.telegeography.com/
products/commsupdate/
articles/2013/01/03/
huawei-bags-guinean-
backbone-contract-sotelgui-
rescue-plans-ongoing/.

"The African Startup Using Phones
to Spot Counterfeit Drugs."
Bloomberg, July 31, 2015.
www.bloomberg.com/news/
features/2015-07-31/the-african-
startup-using-phones-to-spot-
counterfeit-drugs.

Thede, Nancy. "Policy Coherence for
Development and Securitisation:
Competing Paradigms or
Stabilising North–South
Hierarchies?" *Third World
Quarterly* 34, no. 5 (2013): 784–799.

Tilouine, Joan, and Ghalia Kadiri.
"A Addis-Abeba, le siège de
l'Union africaine espionné par
Pékin." *Le Monde*, January 26,
2018. www.lemonde.fr/afrique/
article/2018/01/26/a-addis-
abeba-le-siege-de-l-union-
africaine-espionne-par-les-
chinois_5247521_3212.html.

Tsui, Benjamin. "Do Huawei's
Training Programs and Centers
Transfer Skills to Africa?" China
Africa Research Initiative.
Johns Hopkins, 2016. http://
static1.squarespace.com/
static/5652847de4b033f5
6d2bdc29/t/578e94e83e00b
e65954feb3f/1468962026573/
Tsui+brief+v.5.pdf.

Tsui, Lokman. "An Inadequate
Metaphor: The Great Firewall
and Chinese Internet

Censorship." *Global Dialogue* 9,
no. 1/2 (2007): 60.
———. "Internet Opening up China:
Fact or Fiction." In *Media in
Transition: Globalization &
Convergence Conference*, 10–12.
MIT Press, 2002.

Turse, Nick. "How the NSA Built a
Secret Surveillance Network
for Ethiopia." *The Intercept*,
September 13, 2017. https://
theintercept.com/2017/09/13/
nsa-ethiopia-surveillance-
human-rights/.

Umejei, Emeka. "Hybridizing
Journalism: Clash of Two
'Journalisms' in Africa." *Chinese
Journal of Communication*,
May 18, 2018, 1–15. https://doi.
org/10.1080/17544750.
2018.1473266.

UN Security Council. Resolution 1373
(2001).

UNECA. *The African Information
Society Initiative: A Decade's
Perspective*. UNECA, 2008.

US Embassy in Addis Ababa.
"Wikileaks Cable
#09ADDISABABA149," 2009.

USAID. "USAID/Leland Initiative
Home Page," November 9, 2001.
https://web.archive.
org/web/20011109164754/http://
www.usaid.gov/leland/.

Vaughan, Sarah, and Mesfin
Gebremichael. "Rethinking
Business and Politics in
Ethiopia." *Africa Power and
Politics, UK Aid, Irish Aid*, 2011.

Voice of America. "Ethiopian PM
Defends Anti-Terror Law,

Condemns Critics." *VOA*, 2012. www.voanews.com/a/ethiopian-pm-defends-anti-terror-law-condemns-critics-138976759/159572.html.

Wa Kuhenga, Makwaia. "The Alliance between Tanzania's CCM and China's CPC." *China Daily*, 2017. http://wap.chinadaily.com.cn/2017-03/24/content_28664166.htm.

Wahito, Margaret. "Kenya: China to Fund Kenya's Fibre Optic Project." *Capital FM*. June 28, 2012. http://allafrica.com/stories/201206290024.html.

Wainaina, Binyavanga. "How to Write about Africa." *Granta Magazine*, January 19, 2006. https://granta.com/how-to-write-about-africa/.

Wang, C. "Concerning the Development and Administration of Our Country's Internet." *China Rights Forum* 2 (2010). www.hrichina.org/en/content/3241.

"WCIT: National Governments' Control over the Internet May Be a Side-Effect." *Infosecurity Magazine*, December 6, 2012. www.infosecurity-magazine.com:443/news/wcit-national-governments-control-over-the/.

Webster, Frank. *Theories of the Information Society*. Routledge, 2014.

Wei, Lu. "Cyber Sovereignty Must Rule Global Internet." *Huffington Post*, December 15, 2014. www.huffingtonpost.com/lu-wei/china-cyber-sovereignty_b_6324060.html.

Wekesa, Bob. "Emerging Trends and Patterns in China–Africa Media Dynamics: A Discussion from an East African Perspective." *Ecquid Novi: African Journalism Studies* 34, no. 3 (2013): 62–78.

"Who's Afraid of Huawei?" *The Economist*, August 4, 2012. www.economist.com/node/21559922.

Wolf, David. *Making the Connection: The Peaceful Rise of China's Telecommunications Giants*. Wolf Group Asia, 2012.

World Bank. "Fact Sheet: Infrastructure in Sub-Saharan Africa." *World Bank*, 2010. http://go.worldbank.org/SWDECPM5S0.

Wu, Yu-Shan. *The Rise of China's State-Led Media Dynasty in Africa*. South African Institute of International Affairs, 2012.

Xin, Xin. "Xinhua News Agency in Africa." *Journal of African Media Studies* 1, no. 3 (2009): 363–377.

Xinhua. "China Extends Economic Assistance to Zimbabwe." *Xinhua*, April 7, 2012. www.focac.org/eng/zxxx/ t925720.htm.

———. "Visiting Chinese Commerce Minister Signs Agreements with Zimbabwe." *Xinhua*, February 22, 2013. www.china.org.cn/world/Off_the_Wire/2013-02/22/content_28036524.htm.

Xinhua News Agency. "China Headlines: Xi Slams 'Double Standards,' Advocates Shared Future in Cyberspace." *Xinhua*, December

16, 2015. http://news.xinhuanet.
com/english/indepth/2015-
12/16/c_134924012.htm.

Yan, Li. "Reforming Internet
Governance and the Role of
China." Focus Asia, Institute
for Security and Development
Policy, Stockholm 7 (2015).
http://isdp.eu/content/uploads/
publications/2015-LiYan-
Reforming-Internet-Governance-
and-the-role-of-China.pdf.

Yang, Guobin. *The Power of the
Internet in China: Citizen
Activism Online.* Columbia
University Press, 2013.

Yanqiu, Zhang, and Simon
Matingwina. "Constructive
Journalism: A New Journalistic
Paradigm of Chinese Media in
Africa." In *China's Media and Soft
Power in Africa*, 93–105. Palgrave
Series in Asia and Pacific Studies.
Palgrave Macmillan, 2016. https://
doi.org/10.1057/9781137539670_7.

Yardley, Jim. "Snubbed by U.S.,
China Finds New Space
Partners." *The New York
Times*, May 24, 2007, sec.
International/Asia Pacific. www.
nytimes.com/2007/05/24/
world/asia/24satellite.html.

York, Geoffrey. "Why China Is
Making a Big Play to Control
Africa's Media." *The Globe and
Mail*, September 11, 2013. www.
theglobeandmail.com/news/
world/media-agenda-china-buys-
newsrooms-influence-in-africa/
article14269323/.

Zeng, Jinghan, and Shaun Breslin.
"China's 'New Type of Great
Power Relations': A G2 with
Chinese Characteristics?"
International Affairs 92, no. 4
(2016): 773–794.

Zeng, Jinghan, Tim Stevens, and Yaru
Chen. "China's Solution to Global
Cyber Governance: Unpacking
the Domestic Discourse of
'Internet Sovereignty.'" *Politics &
Policy* 45, no. 3 (2017): 432–464.

Zhang, Bing. "Understanding
China's Telecommunications
Policymaking and Reforms:
A Tale of Transition toward
Liberalization." *Telematics and
Informatics* 19, no. 4 (2002):
331–349.

Zhang, Xiaoling. "How Ready Is China
for a China-Style World Order?
China's State Media Discourse
under Construction." *Ecquid
Novi: African Journalism
Studies* 34, no. 3 (2013):
79–101.

Zhao, Yuezhi. *Communication
in China: Political Economy,
Power, and Conflict.* Rowman &
Littlefield, 2008.

———. "The State, the Market, and
Media Control in China." In
Who Owns the Media, edited
by Zaharom Nain and Pradip
Thomas. Zed Books, 2004.

———. "Understanding China's
Media System in a World
Historical Context." *Comparing
Media Systems beyond the
Western World*, 2012, 143–173.

INDEX

Note: Page numbers followed by *n* indicate an endnote with relevant number.

ZED

Zed is a platform for marginalised voices across the globe.

It is the world's largest publishing collective and a world leading example of alternative, non-hierarchical business practice.

It has no CEO, no MD and no bosses and is owned and managed by its workers who are all on equal pay.

It makes its content available in as many languages as possible.

It publishes content critical of oppressive power structures and regimes.

It publishes content that changes its readers' thinking.

It publishes content that other publishers won't and that the establishment finds threatening.

It has been subject to repeated acts of censorship by states and corporations.

It fights all forms of censorship.

It is financially and ideologically independent of any party, corporation, state or individual.

Its books are shared all over the world.

www.zedbooks.net
@ZedBooks